100 Life-Changing Tips
Using Microsoft Office for Windows

THE must-have skills to deliver better results in less time

Vickie Sokol Evans, MCT

100 Life-Changing Tips Using Microsoft Office for Windows

By Vickie Sokol Evans

Copyright © 2019 by Vickie Sokol Evans, MCT and The Red Cape Company, LLC. All rights reserved. No part of the contents of this manual may be printed, reproduced, or transmitted in any form or by any means electronic or mechanical, including photocopying, recording, or by any information storage or retrieval system without written permission from The Red Cape Company, except for the inclusion of brief quotations or review.

PUBLISHED BY
The Red Cape Company
9901 Brodie Lane, Suite 160-225
Austin, TX 78748

support@redcapeco.com | www.redcapeco.com/100tips

Author: Vickie Sokol Evans, MCT

Microsoft, Microsoft Press, Access, ActiveX, Edge, Excel, Expression, Groove, InfoPath, Internet Explorer, OneDrive, OneNote, OpenType, Outlook, PivotTable, PowerPoint, SharePoint, SmartArt, Teams, Visio, Windows, Windows Server, and Office 365 are either registered trademarks or trademarks of the Microsoft group of companies. Other product and company names, such as PepsiCo and Hyatt Regency among others, mentioned herein are the trademarks of their respective owners. Dunder Mifflin fictional paper company employees used in examples are characters from NBC Universal's television show *The Office*.

Other example companies, organizations, products, domain names, email addresses, logos, people, places, and events depicted herein are fictitious. No association with any real company, organization, product, domain name, email address, logo, person, place, or event is intended or should be inferred.

This manual expresses the author's views and opinions. The information contained in this manual is provided without any express, statutory, or implied warranties. Neither the author, The Red Cape Company, nor its resellers, or distributors will be held liable for any damages caused or alleged to be caused either directly or indirectly by this manual.

Information contained in this manual has been obtained by The Red Cape Company from sources believed to be reliable. However, because of the possibility of error by our sources, The Red Cape Company, or others, do not guarantee the accuracy, adequacy, or completeness of any information and is not responsible for any errors or omissions or the results obtained from use of such information. Readers should be particularly aware of the fact that the Internet and software are both ever-changing entities. Some facts, images, and step by step instructions may have changed since this manual went to press.

© 2019 Vickie Sokol Evans, MCT; The Red Cape Company, LLC. All Rights Reserved.

Get the bonus video and sample files!

Want to see the tips in action? Visit www.redcapeco.com/bonus-vids to see Vickie walk through Excel tips such as conditional formatting and other important digital productivity tricks that will help you reveal critical information about your data!

We'll also send you sample files so you can test the tips and practice your new skills.

© 2019 Vickie Sokol Evans, MCT; The Red Cape Company, LLC. All Rights Reserved.

Dedication

To Sokol and Will who inspire me every day.

To my mother who instilled in me a love for technology and to my father who is MY hero.

To the dozens of superheroes sitting in front of a document, spreadsheet, presentation, or their inbox at this very minute thinking, "There has to be a better way!"

© 2019 Vickie Sokol Evans, MCT; The Red Cape Company, LLC. All Rights Reserved.

Contents

How to use this book i

    Multi-version support i

Chapter 1: Windows Tips 1

    Look, Ma! No mouse 1

    Tip #1   Save time (and your sanity) by using essential Windows keyboard shortcuts 2

    Tip #2   Snap windows side by side 3

    Tip #3   Quickly launch a program 3

    Tip #4   Switch between open windows 4

    Find things faster. 6

    Tip #5   Quickly find documents and files using the Start Menu or Windows Explorer 6

    Tip #6   Discover and ask for relevant information using Cortana 9

    Personalize your experience. 12

    Tip #7   Add a second (and third!) time zone to your system clock 12

    Tip #8   Pin your favorite apps to the Start Menu 14

    Tip #9   Create shortcuts to your favorite files and folders 14

    Tip #10   Move, group, and name tiles 16

Chapter 2: Microsoft Office Tips 19

    Access your work anywhere, anytime, on any device. 19

    Tip #11   Connect your cloud-based storage drives to Microsoft Office 19

    Tip #12   Save your files to the cloud for anytime, anywhere access using OneDrive 23

    Work together effectively. 28

    Tip #13   Share files with others effortlessly 28

    Tip #14   Find a file shared with you (so you don't have to ask for it again!) 35

    Tip #15   Edit a document with a colleague at the same time 39

    Tip #16   Collaborate with colleagues using interactive comments 41

    Improve your workflow across all programs 43

    Tip #17   Pin your favorite documents to the Open screen 43

    Tip #18   Create your own toolbar using the Quick Access Toolbar 44

    Tip #19   Create your own Ribbon 46

    Tip #20   Use the Tell Me feature to get things done faster 53

© 2019 Vickie Sokol Evans, MCT; The Red Cape Company, LLC. All Rights Reserved.

Instantly brand your documents, spreadsheets, and presentations......................................56

Tip #21 Change the color palette for text, tables, and other objects 56

Tip #22 Globally change the font used in your document 58

Tip #23 Brand your documents using Themes 60

Manage your file behind the scenes. 62

Tip #24 Create, email, and convert PDFs 62

Tip #25 Remove personal data (aka Metadata)...64

Chapter 3: Microsoft Word Tips 69

Save hours of formatting time. 69

Tip #26 Discover selecting tricks using the document margin.................................69

Tip #27 Use Styles to format your document..70

Tip #28 Use F4 to repeat last action..71

Tip #29 Select all text with similar formatting 72

Tip #30 Reformat your document in seconds using Style Sets 73

Tip #31 Modify a style..74

Tip #32 Create a table of contents in seconds 75

Tip #33 Create a professional cover page in an instant 78

Work like a pro. 79

Tip #34 Add letters from a foreign alphabet 79

Tip #35 Find and replace special characters 79

Effortlessly design and manage tables 83

Tip #36 Format a table in seconds 83

Tip #37 Effortlessly move table rows 84

Tip #38 Confidently delete a table 84

Navigate quickly throughout your document.... 85

Tip #39 Use your headings and keyboard shortcuts to navigate your document 85

Tip #40 Easily move content like never before..86

Chapter 4: Microsoft Excel Tips 89

Save time using "back to basics" tools. 89

Tip #41 Discover Autofill tips to save data entry time and prevent mistakes 89

Tip #42 Quickly select your data.. 93

Tip #43 Use AutoFit to resize columns and rows...94

Tip #44 Instantly add today's date and time using keyboard shortcuts......................95

Manage your data with minimal effort. 96

Tip #45 Format a list as a table 96

Tip #46 Expand the table as you type 98

© 2019 Vickie Sokol Evans, MCT; The Red Cape Company. All Rights Reserved.

Tip #47	Create a calculated column with minimal effort	100
Tip #48	Instantly add a total row to your table	101
Tip #49	Use Slicers to quickly filter your table	102
Tip #50	Effortlessly select and move columns	104
Tip #51	Remove duplicate records	105
Tip #52	Summarize your data using a PivotTable	106

Save time and reduce errors using magical tools. **109**

Tip #53	Fix formatting issues using Clear Formats	109
Tip #54	Quickly sum or count a range of cells (and show off your math skills!)	110
Tip #55	Use Text to Columns to separate First and Last columns from a Full Name column	111
Tip #56	Use Flash Fill to separate, combine, and create columns of data	115
Tip #57	Use the Paste Special feature to perform magic and transform your data	116

Reveal critical information about your data. **120**

Tip #58	Flag duplicate values in your column	120
Tip #59	Use conditional formatting for Status Flags	123
Tip #60	Use a heat map to track your progress	127
Tip #61	Effortlessly create a chart	128
Tip #62	See the trend in each row using Sparklines	131

Share nicely with others. **134**

Tip #63	Prevent columns from printing across two pages	134
Tip #64	Print column headings to show on each page	136
Tip #65	Send a worksheet – not the entire workbook – to a colleague	137

Chapter References **139**

Chapter 5: Microsoft PowerPoint Tips **141**

Don't reinvent the wheel. **141**

| Tip #66 | Use a Theme to define your colors, fonts, and layouts | 141 |
| Tip #67 | Reuse and merge slides from other presentations | 147 |

Manage your presentation. **148**

Tip #68	Create sections in PowerPoint	148
Tip #69	Use the new Zoom feature to create summary slides and navigation	152
Tip #70	Create one slide show for multiple audiences	156

Work smarter and reduce panic attacks. **158**

Tip #71	Save hours by using layouts	158
Tip #72	Fix a problem slide using the magical Reset button	160
Tip #73	Format multiple slides at once by modifying the layout	161
Tip #74	Create a new slide layout to reduce errors, ensure consistency, and save time	163

© 2019 Vickie Sokol Evans, MCT; The Red Cape Company, LLC. All Rights Reserved.

Be kind to your audience. **168**

Tip #75 Convert boring text to SmartArt 168

Tip #76 Add compelling transitions to your key topic slides.................... 170

Become an instant graphic artist. **172**

Tip #77 Use picture tools to enhance your images.................................. 172

Tip #78 Magically replace an image without affecting other objects and settings 176

Tip #79 Work with objects like the pros 176

Tip #80 Use the new Designer tool to transform a slide 178

Present like the pros. **180**

Tip #81 Use keyboard shortcuts to run your slide show 180

Tip #82 See your notes and next slides while you are presenting 180

Tip #83 Instantly and confidently jump to a slide or section while presenting 185

Tip #84 Zoom in on a slide 185

Tip #85 Use recording tools to effectively communicate your message.................. 186

Chapter 6: Microsoft Outlook Tips 191

Reduce your email volume. **191**

Tip #86 Instantly remove redundant messages using Clean Up 191

Tip #87 Ignore conversations without hurting anyone's feelings 197

Tip #88 Reply with a meeting 198

Save time for yourself and others. **200**

Tip #89 Reduce time zone errors 200

Tip #90 Create one-click links for mobile users 203

Tip #91 Effortlessly work with attachments... 206

Tip #92 Use @mentions to improve communication and save time 210

Tip #93 Avoid embarrassing mistakes when repurposing and resending messages.......... 212

Tip #94 Use fancy email options to set your mail to expire and redirect replies 215

Find email fast. **219**

Tip #95 Quickly search for email using the powerful Search Bar 219

Tip #96 Create dynamic Search Folders to return to frequent searches 221

Automate your work. **226**

Tip #97 Use conditional formatting to highlight messages from VIPs........ 226

Tip #98 Create rules to process and reroute messages 229

Tip #99 Use Quick Steps to automate multi-step processes 235

Tip #100 Create automatic responses and links to websites using Quick Parts 242

© 2019 Vickie Sokol Evans, MCT; The Red Cape Company. All Rights Reserved.

Appendix... **249**

List of Figures 249

© 2019 Vickie Sokol Evans, MCT; The Red Cape Company, LLC. All Rights Reserved.

How to use this book

Multi-version support

Thank you for purchasing this book! It is my hope that these tips will help you execute flawlessly so that you can focus on what matters most to you. Whether it's delivering better results faster, saving time so that you can finally get to volleyball practice, or simply wanting more out of your technology, this book will give you valuable best practices and practical tips that you can use immediately. Even better, you don't need to purchase a new book every time you upgrade or anytime Microsoft updates the software. These tips apply to most versions of Windows and Microsoft Office and they include the essential tips everyone should master.

However, it is important to note that I wrote this edition of the book using Windows 10 and Microsoft Office 365 Version 1905 Build 11629.20196. If a tip has completely different steps for a previous version, then I added them at the end of the tip. Therefore, if the steps or screenshots are a little off compared to your version, look for the extra instructions at the end of a tip. To better understand this, review the framework I followed as outlined on the right.

I hope you enjoy the book! Email
support@redcapeco.com if you have any
feedback for me.

<mark>Highlighted Margins</mark> **Highlighted margins.** A yellow-highlighted margin indicates when a tip meets an objective of a Microsoft Office Specialist (MOS) certification exam. <mark>Green highlight</mark> applies to Expert-Level exams objectives

© 2019 Vickie Sokol Evans, MCT The Red Cape Company. All Rights Reserved.

Icons used in this book

Highlight this. You may want to refer back to it later.

Look closely. Here is a behind-the-scenes look at this tip. Read on for helpful information about the tip.

More information. There's more information you need to know to help you as you read further.

Reuse, Repeat, or Repurpose. Repeat the steps as necessary or reuse the tip for other tasks.

Stop. In the name of love! If you go any further bad things might happen, so follow the steps provided to help you avoid a problem.

Save time. There's an even quicker way to use this tip.

Setting. This provides information required for a specific setting within the application.

Microsoft Office 2010. The steps are different for previous versions. Follow these steps if you are using Microsoft Office 2010

Microsoft Office 2013. The steps are different for previous versions. Follow these steps if you are using Microsoft Office 2013

MOS objective. The tip meets an objective of a Microsoft Office Specialist (MOS) certification exam.

Let's begin.

Chapter 1: Windows Tips

Save time, secure your information, stay organized, search effectively, and work efficiently.

In this Chapter

- Navigate around and manage your computer at the press of a button
- Find folders, documents, and apps faster than ever
- Create shortcuts to your favorite programs and files
- Set up your workspace to boost your productivity

Look, Ma! No mouse.

Many of the tips in this section use a special button on the keyboard known as the Windows logo key, seen in Figure 1 below.

Figure 1. Windows logo key on a standard keyboard

 The Windows logo key will be referred to as the [WINDOWS] key.

© 2019 Vickie Sokol Evans, MCT; The Red Cape Company, LLC. All Rights Reserved.

Tip #1   Save time (and your sanity) by using essential Windows keyboard shortcuts

Applies to most versions of Windows

Yes! That floating Windows logo key button on your keyboard actually serves a purpose. Check out these timesaving (and cool!) shortcuts you won't want to live without.

Action	Keyboard Shortcut	When using a mouse
View Explorer Window ("My Computer" window)	[WINDOWS]+[E]	Right-click the Start button. Then choose FILE EXPLORER.
View Desktop	[WINDOWS]+[D]	Right-click the Start button. Then choose DESKTOP.
View the Start Menu	[WINDOWS] Key	Click the Start button.
View all open windows	[WINDOWS]+[TAB]	Click TASK VIEW, the third icon on the Taskbar (to the right of the Windows icon).
Lock the computer	[WINDOWS]+[L]	Press [CTRL]+[ALT]+[DELETE] and then click LOCK.
Search for everything!	[WINDOWS]+[S]	Click CORTANA, the second icon on the Taskbar (to the right of the Windows icon).
Connect to a projector	[WINDOWS]+[P]	

2   © 2019 Vickie Sokol Evans, MCT; The Red Cape Company. All Rights Reserved.

Tip #2   Snap windows side by side

Introduced in Windows 7

In previous versions of Windows, when you want to view two windows side by side (such as when you need to view a spreadsheet and a Word document at the same time) you would have to resize each window individually. Windows 7 introduced a new feature called Snap that allows you to drag the title bar of a window all the way to either side of your screen and it will snap to that half of the screen. An even quicker way to snap your window to the side is to use a keyboard shortcut.

You can use this feature with any window, including internet browsers, apps, files and Explorer windows.

To view windows side by side using Snap

1. Click in the window you want to snap to the left to make sure it is the current active window.
2. Use the [WINDOWS]+[LEFT ARROW] keyboard shortcut to snap the current window to the left side of the screen.
3. Windows 10 will showcase all open files in the right side of your screen. Go ahead and select one of the open files to snap a document to the right side of your screen.
4. If Windows doesn't showcase all your open files, then click in the window of the document you want to snap to the right side of the screen to make sure it is the current active window.
5. Use the [WINDOWS]+[RIGHT ARROW] keyboard shortcut to snap the current window to the right.

 Test out what the other arrow keys do using the Snap feature. With the [WINDOWS] key pressed, cycle through the up, down, right, and left arrows.

Tip #3   Quickly launch a program

Applies to Windows 7, Windows 10

Now that you've learned about the [WINDOWS] key, check out how easy it is to launch programs.

To quickly launch a program

1. Press the [WINDOWS] Key. This launches the Windows 10 Start Screen as seen in Figure 2.

Figure 2. Window 10 Start Screen

2. Next, simply start typing the program you want – such as **Calculator** or **Snipping Tool** or **Outlook** or **OneNote** or **Clock** – and the Search pane will display possible matches.
3. Hit the [ENTER] key to launch the app. It's like magic!

 You can use this trick to launch all sorts of things: Games folder (type: **games**), your Printers window (type: **printer**), your music folder (type: **music**), your display settings (type: **display** or type: **resolution**) and much more...

Tip #4   Switch between open windows

Applies to all versions of Windows

At any given point throughout the day, you probably have many apps and windows open. You can easily switch between them using a keyboard shortcut.

To cycle through all open windows using your keyboard

- You can cycle through open windows by holding down the [ALT] key and pressing [TAB], [TAB], [TAB]... until you land on the window you want.

© 2019 Vickie Sokol Evans, MCT; The Red Cape Company. All Rights Reserved.

To toggle back and forth between two windows

■ You can toggle back and forth between two windows by pressing [ALT]+[TAB] once, and then repeat. This takes you to the previous window you were using. Press [ALT]+[TAB] again and it takes you back to the other window. Repeat as necessary.

To view all of the open applications

■ To view all open windows, use the keyboard shortcut [WINDOWS]+[TAB].

Find things faster.

Tip #5   Quickly find documents and files using the Start Menu or Windows Explorer

Applies to Windows 7, Windows 10

Ever have trouble remembering where you saved that critical file, folder, or document? Thankfully, you no longer need to remember where you saved files in your various folders. Windows Search allows you to find more things faster than ever before.

You have two options: the Start Menu and Windows Explorer.

To quickly find documents and other files using the Start Menu

Suppose I'm looking for documents related to my client Contoso. Searching using the Start Menu will find all files with Contoso in the name of the file as well as Contoso within the document – either as content or as metadata.

For more information about Metadata, see Tip #25.

1. Use the [WINDOWS] key to launch the Start Menu.
2. Type the content you're looking for. For me, I typed **Contoso**. By default, the search results list displays files where Contoso is in the name of the file as seen in Figure 3.

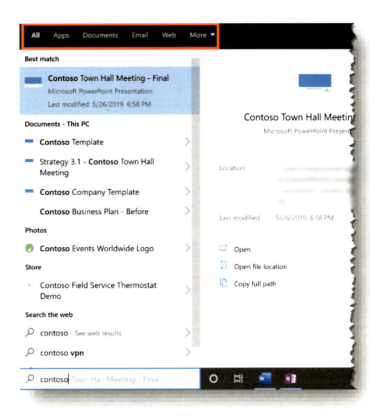

Figure 3. Default Search Results

3. To see more files based on your search criteria, click the **DOCUMENTS** button at the top of the Search screen and Windows Search will display all files where the search term is in the name of the file as well as within the document – either as content or as metadata.

To search your computer using Windows Explorer

Use Windows Explorer as your search tool when you want to manage the scope of the search and/or use advanced search criteria. For instance, I have an image of Dwight Schrute that I use for training purposes. It's located somewhere in my content library in SharePoint, which is synced to my computer.

1. Use the keyboard shortcut [WINDOWS]+[E] to launch an Explorer window. See Tip #1 for more info about the [WINDOWS] Key.
2. Click on the drive, folder, or subfolder where you want to search. For instance, the C:/ Drive. I will click on The Red Cape Company's SharePoint directory as seen highlighted by the number (1) in Figure 4.
3. Use [CTRL]+[F] keyboard shortcut to go to the Search field, which also activates the **SEARCH TOOLS** ribbon.
4. Type your search term. In this example, we'll use **Schrute** as seen highlighted by the number (2) in Figure 4. Windows will find all documents

in the SharePoint libraries that are currently syncing to my computer where the search term is in the name of the file, as seen in Figure 4.

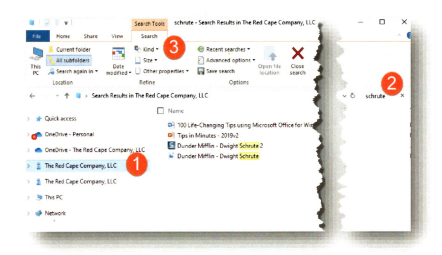

Figure 4. Search results from Windows Explorer

Note: Windows Explorer search method **does not** search for the word Schrute in documents. It only searches for files with the search term in the name of the file.

5. You can narrow down your search by clicking any of the properties in the **REFINE** group on the ribbon, such as **DATE MODIFIED** or **KIND** of file, such as an image or document or folder as seen in Figure 4 (3).

To quickly search your computer for the largest files

Oh no! It looks like I'm running out of room on my hard drive. I'm going to fix this using Windows Explorer as my search tool to find the largest files on my computer.

1. Use the keyboard shortcut [WINDOWS]+[E] to launch an Explorer window. See Tip #1 for more info about the [WINDOWS] Key.
2. Click on the drive, folder, or subfolder where you want to search. For instance, the C:/ Drive.
3. Use [CTRL]+[F] keyboard shortcut to go to the Search field, which also activates the **SEARCH TOOLS** ribbon.
4. On the **SEARCH TOOLS** ribbon, in the **REFINE** group, click the **SIZE** drop town and choose **GIGANTIC** (as seen in Figure 5) to find the largest files on your computer across all folders.

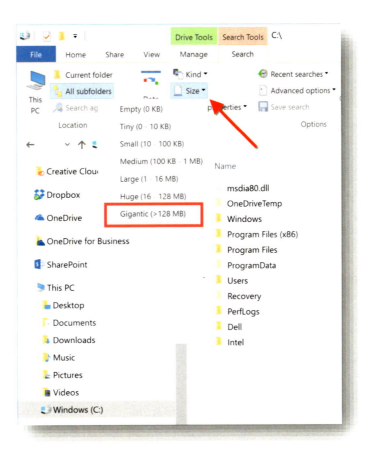

Figure 5. Use Windows Explorer to find the largest files on your computer.

Tip #6   Discover and ask for relevant information using Cortana
New in Windows 10

Cortana, Microsoft's personal assistant, can help you instantly get the information you need throughout your day. Just ask her!

How to get the information you need by asking Cortana

1. Say "Hey Cortana!"

   If Cortana doesn't respond when you say "Hey Cortana" that feature may be turned off or disabled. Follow the steps below to customize Cortana's preferences.

2. After you say "Hey Cortana" and she wakes up, ask her your question, such as:

   - o "What time zone is Nashville in?"
   - o "How do you spell pneumonia?"

© 2019 Vickie Sokol Evans, MCT; The Red Cape Company, LLC. All Rights Reserved.   9

- "Convert 49.95 U.S. dollars to British pounds."
- "What currency do they use in Sweden?"
- "Where is the nearest pharmacy?"

Ask Cortana anything! Talking to a computer may feel weird at first, but it's a fun and easy way to get the information you need.

To customize Cortana's preferences

1. Launch Cortana by clicking Cortana's icon on the Start menu task bar as seen in Figure 6.

Figure 6. Start menu task bar

2. This is Cortana's home where relevant information will be displayed for you.
3. Click the Notebook icon as seen highlighted by the number (1) in Figure 7 and then personalize your experience.
4. Click the Gear icon as seen highlighted by the number (2) Figure 7 to modify additional settings, including how to get Cortana to respond to "Hey Cortana."

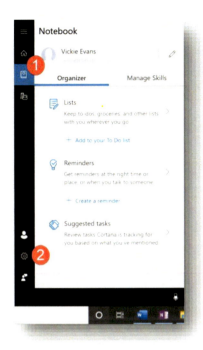

Figure 7. Cortana Notebook options

Personalize your experience.

Tip #7   Add a second (and third!) time zone to your system clock
New in Windows 10

When you have a team that works in different time zones it helps to be able to quickly see what time it is for them right now. In Windows 10, you can hover over your system clock to view not only your local time, but also up to two more time zones. As seen in Figure 8, I added two additional time zones for my colleagues on the East Coast and in London.

Figure 8. Windows 10 system clock with two additional time zones.

How to add a second (and third!) time zone to your system clock

1. Launch the Start Menu by using your [WINDOWS] key as described in Tip #3 on page 3.
2. Type **time** in the Start Menu text box to search for the **Date & Time settings** and hit [ENTER].
3. Look for the setting "Add clocks for different time zones," as seen in Figure 9.

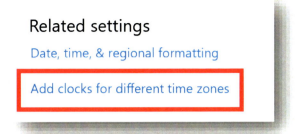

Figure 9. "Add clocks for different time zones" Setting

4. Configure the additional clocks as seen in Figure 10.

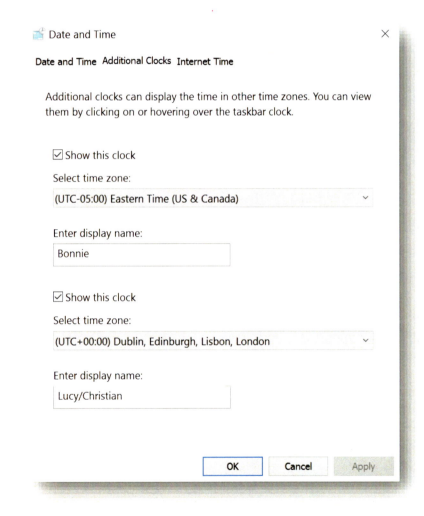

Figure 10. Additional Clocks dialog box.

Tip #8   Pin your favorite apps to the Start Menu

Applies to Windows 10

In previous version of Windows, the Start Menu was a list of applications and tools that served as a launching pad. New in Windows 10, the Start Menu includes Tiles, which provide more real estate and a fully customizable user experience. Follow these instructions to create your own unique Start Menu.

How to pin your favorite apps to the Start Menu

Stop: Do not launch the app. Just find it.

1. Find the application you wish to pin to the Start Menu using one of the following two methods:
   - Launch the Start Menu in Windows 10 and scroll through the list of apps on the left side of the Start Menu
     or…
   - (**Recommended**) Press the [WINDOWS] Key and start typing the application you want, such as **Outlook** or **Skype** or **OneNote**.
2. Using your mouse, right-click the application you wish to make a shortcut for.
3. Then click **PIN TO START**. The app is now added to the Start Menu. See Tip #10 to learn how to move and group your apps on your Start Menu.

To unpin from the Start Menu. Repeat the same steps to unpin programs you don't want on the Start Menu.

To pin your favorite program to the Taskbar on your Desktop

1. Repeat steps 1-2 above.
2. Then click **PIN TO TASKBAR**.

Tip #9   Create shortcuts to your favorite files and folders

Applies to Windows 10

In the previous step, you added your favorite apps to the Start Screen. The next step is to add your favorite files and folders, which is extremely helpful for those active project files or files that you access monthly or quarterly.

To pin your favorite folders to your Start Screen

1. Navigate to your folder you want to add to the Start Menu. Hint: use [WINDOWS]+[E].
2. Using your mouse, right-click the folder to get the command menu or using your touch screen, tap and hold to get the command menu.
3. Click or tap **PIN TO START**.

To pin your favorite files to your Start Screen

1. Open the file you want to save to your Start Screen so that it shows up in the most recent files list for that application. For instance, open your favorite spreadsheet in Excel. You can close the file.
2. Make sure Excel is already pinned to the Start menu, see Tip #8 on how to do that.
3. Right-click the Excel tile on the Start menu and locate the file in the recent list of files as seen in Figure 11. This is called the Jump List.

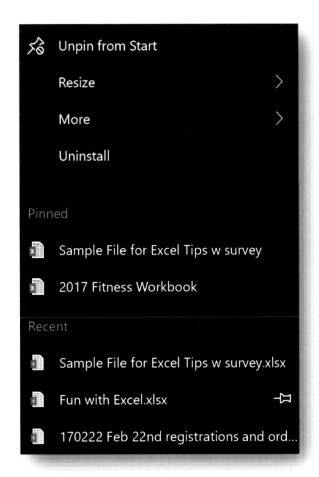

Figure 11. Excel Jump List on the Start Menu

4. Hover on the name of the file and you'll see a pin to the right of the file name. Click the Pin to save it in the Jump List.
5. To access the shortcut, use the [WINDOWS] key to open the Start menu and right-click the Excel app to view the Jump List, which should have your newly pinned file.

 Repeat these same steps for Word and PowerPoint.

Tip #10   Move, group, and name tiles

Applies to Windows 10

Now that you've added your favorite apps and folders, it's time to move them around, group, and rename them. That way, you can customize your Start Screen just the way you want it.

To customize the Start Menu, you must always be on the Start Menu.

To move tiles around the Start Menu

- Drag and drop a tile to the desired location.

To create a new group of tiles

1. Using your mouse, drag and drop a tile to a blank area of the Start Menu.
2. Add more tiles next to the first tile.
3. Give your group of tiles a name by placing your mouse towards the top of the group. You will see "Name group" at the top left-hand side of Figure 12.

Figure 12. Naming your new group of tiles on the Start Menu

4. Click in the "Name group" area and type a new name.

5. Hit [Enter].

To move groups

- Click and hold the title bar of your group and drag the group of tiles to the new location.

Chapter 2: Microsoft Office Tips

Customize and use timesaving features across all Microsoft Office programs: collaborate with your colleagues, manage document properties, and easily brand your documents.

In this Chapter

- Create timesaving shortcuts to improve your effectiveness throughout all Microsoft Office programs
- Use Themes to quickly create impressive and professional-looking branded deliverables
- Create, email and convert PDFs
- Work in your documents at the same time with your colleagues
- Save valuable time by using the latest features of Microsoft Office

Access your work anywhere, anytime, on any device.

Tip #11   Connect your cloud-based storage drives to Microsoft Office

Applies to Office 365

What kind of superhuman benefit is there to signing in to Microsoft Office? Well, just like those famous superheroes, you get to work whenever and wherever you want because all that you really need is always ready!

Signing in to Microsoft Office allows you to save your Office files securely online in OneDrive or SharePoint. This lets you access them anywhere, anytime and share securely with anyone. Even better, your documents travel with you no matter where you need them—even across different devices, including your mobile phone!

There are three types of accounts for Office 365: Work, School and Personal.

	Type	Description
1	Work	When using Office 365 at work, you will use your work email address to log into Office 365 in order to connect to your cloud-based OneDrive and SharePoint libraries.

© 2019 Vickie Sokol Evans, MCT; The Red Cape Company, LLC. All Rights Reserved. 19

	Type	Description
2	School	When your school issues you an Office 365 account, you will use your school-issued email address to log into Office 365 in order to connect your cloud-based file locations.
3	Personal	Personal accounts are referred to as Microsoft accounts. You'll need a Microsoft ID to log into your Office 365 apps on your computer or device to access your personal files in OneDrive. A Microsoft ID can be your Xbox account, Hotmail, Outlook, or Live email address. If you don't have any of those, you can create a Microsoft ID using any personal email address, including Gmail!

To sign in to Microsoft Office

1. The first time you launch Microsoft Office, you will be prompted to sign in. Type the email address associated with your work, school, or personal Microsoft account.
2. Once signed in, your name will display in the upper right-hand corner of the program window near the Minimize, Restore and Exit buttons as seen in Figure 13. In my example, I'm signed in using my work account.

Figure 13. My name in the top right-hand corner of my application window indicates I'm logged into Office 365.

3. Click your name to view the account(s). Similar to Figure 14, you should be able to see how you're signed into Office 365 and have the ability to view your Office 365 account online and your info within the desktop app.

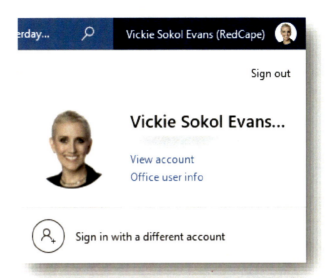

Figure 14. The Office 365 account profile screen within Microsoft Office

4. To view your storage drives for your connected accounts, go to the **FILE** tab and click **ACCOUNT** or click on your name in the top right-hand corner of the app and select **OFFICE USER INFO**.
5. Under **CONNECTED SERVICES**, you will see the work-related cloud-based drives such as OneDrive for Business and SharePoint, as well as personal OneDrive accounts if you're logged into your personal Microsoft account as well. See Figure 15.

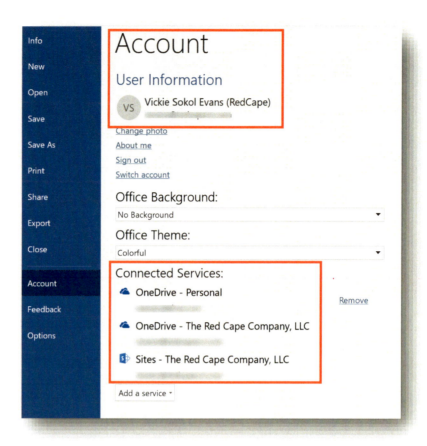

Figure 15. Connected Services using your Microsoft Office account(s)

To sign into Microsoft Office at home

1. The first time you launch Microsoft Office at home, you will be prompted to sign in using your Microsoft ID, which is the same Microsoft ID you used to purchase Office 365.
2. To view your connected account and storage drives, go to the **FILE** tab and click **Open** or use the keyboard shortcut [COMMAND]+[O].
3. Click your image or your name to see the connected services. Because you have Office 365, you should automatically see your personal OneDrive folder listed.

Tip #12   Save your files to the cloud for anytime, anywhere access using OneDrive

Applies to Office 365

When you need access to a document or important presentation, there's nothing more frustrating than realizing that you must be on a specific computer to get that file. Never fear, OneDrive is here!

OneDrive gives you secure cloud-based file storage so that you're never without your files. Additionally, you'll be able to share those files and collaborate easily using the familiar Office applications.

For your personal files, your personal Microsoft ID will give you access to your own secure, cloud-based OneDrive account with plenty of storage space. Additionally, if you are using Office 365 at work, you also have OneDrive for Business, which is where you store all your work files in the cloud. For more information, visit OneDrive.com.

Regardless of whether you use your own OneDrive account or OneDrive for Business, both OneDrive locations are better alternatives than saving to the Desktop, Documents folder, or Network folder because when you save to OneDrive you can access the files from any device, including your mobile phone! In fact, you *must* save your files to the cloud in order to access them from any device. When you save to Documents and Desktop, you cannot access the files when you're away from your computer.

Let's examine the locations I use to save *my* files.

Figure 16. Office 2016 Save Locations

	Command	Description
1	OneDrive – The Red Cape Company, LLC	This is my OneDrive for Business account where I can save all my work-related files in the cloud that I may (or may not) share with my colleagues who are internal to my company.
2	Sites – The Red Cape Company, LLC	This is my corporate SharePoint account where I can save my documents to a Files library in Teams or specific Team Sites on my company's Intranet. These are files that belong to a project or team.
3	OneDrive – Personal	This is where I save all my personal files as well as any files that I want to share externally with my vendors or collaborators. It's similar to a DropBox or

	Command	Description
		Google Drive account but much easier to use because it is integrated with Microsoft Office. Please ask your IT department about your ability to connect your personal OneDrive to your work computer and best practices and protocols for sharing files outside your organization.
4	This PC	This is the native My Computer location where I can save to my Desktop or Documents or even a network drive. This is also where I can access my Google Drive, iCloud Drive, and Drop Box.
5	Add a Place	This is where I added the OneDrive and SharePoint locations I have set up.
6	Browse	If I need to just browse the computer and network drives I have set up, I'll just click Browse and use Windows Explorer to locate the folder where I want to save the document.

To save your files to OneDrive

1. From the **FILE** tab, click **SAVE AS**. Because you have signed in using your Microsoft ID (personal account) or Office 365 account (work/school accounts) in the previous tip, you should see your available locations.
2. If you're saving a personal file, select OneDrive. If you're saving a work file, select OneDrive for Business.
3. Once in your Shared Drive, choose the folder where you want to save your file.
4. Type a file name and then click **Save**. The file(s) will now be accessible on your devices when using the Word, Excel, and PowerPoint mobile apps on your smartphone as seen in Figure 17.

Now that your document is in the cloud, you can access it on any of your devices, such as a tablet or smartphone. If you haven't already, download OneDrive and the Microsoft Office apps to your device(s) and log into Word, Excel, or PowerPoint using your personal Microsoft ID or your work/school email address.

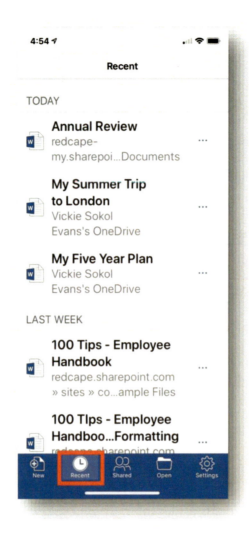

Figure 17. My Recent list in the Word app on my iPhone

Then, when you open Word, Excel, or PowerPoint on your device, your recently saved document will magically appear in the Recent list of the application, as seen in Figure 17. What you see in this screenshot above is a list of the three files I just created as I'm writing this tip. From the laptop I'm using this very minute, I created one work document called "Annual Review" and two personal documents: "My Summer Trip to London" and "My Five Year Plan". As soon as I saved them to their respective cloud locations, I picked up my iPhone and launched the Word app and the three documents magically appeared in the list!

Contact your IT department for more information about the protocol for accessing work files on your devices and personal files on your work laptop.

To open your files from OneDrive

1. From the **FILE** tab, click **OPEN**.
2. As seen in Figure 18, select either OneDrive or OneDrive for Business and navigate to the folder where your document is stored.

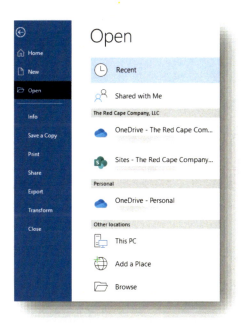

Figure 18. The Open dialog box in Word

Work together effectively.

Collaborate in Office 365 by co-authoring

Many times, we need help from others to complete or review an important document or big presentation. More often than not, we collaborate by sending important files back-and-forth via email. However, the traditional way of emailing the document back and forth is inefficient and can cause delays in getting the project done, not to mention costly mistakes resulting from two or more team members working in separate copies of the document.

Under many of the more traditional methods of file-sharing, it's challenging to know who has the latest version of a particular file and if you're both making changes at the same time. So, whenever you're building documents on a team everyone is potentially doing double work – which means you'll have to invest time comparing documents and merging changes. Just thinking about all that work makes me want to quit the project!

A better, more collaborative way to work together on individual files is to edit the document together at the same time or edit the same exact document at different times. Either way, you and your colleagues are both working in the latest version of the document. This way, you can ensure that any time you access the document, you are in the latest and greatest version. This is called co-authoring.

Prerequisite: The file you and your team are working in together must be stored somewhere in the cloud, such as on SharePoint (your Intranet) or in OneDrive as demonstrated in Tip #12 on page 23. Then, you must share the file as mentioned in Tip #13 on page 28 OR access a file shared with you as described in Tip #14 on page 35.

In Tip #15 on 39, we'll then walk through the steps on how to work together in the same document.

Ready? Let's do this!

Tip #13   Share files with others effortlessly

Applies to Office 365

Want to send your file to a colleague? Consider sending a link to the file instead of sending them a copy of the file so that you're both working in the same document without worrying about who has the latest version. That way, the file will *always* be the latest version!

When your colleague clicks the link you send, the document opens automatically in Word Online, Excel Online, or PowerPoint Online and they can begin reviewing or editing the document depending on the write/read-only permissions you set. If they are on their mobile device, the file opens in the corresponding app associated with the file. It's so easy!

Before we get started, let's first look at the Sharing window for work/school files more closely.

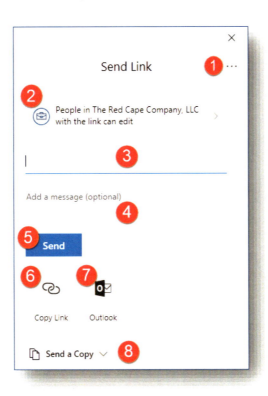

Figure 19. Sharing window in Word (Office 365 for Work/School)

Item	Setting	Description
1	Send Link > Manage Access	View and manage share settings for the document.
2	Link Settings	Change the level of access for the document.
3	Email Address	Enter your colleague's name or email address.
4	Add a message	Draft a short message to the recipient about the shared document you are sending to give them context. This helps the recipient find it when searching their mailbox for the message later.
5	Send	When you're ready to share, hit **SEND**.

Item	Setting	Description
6	Copy Link	If you just need the URL to the document copied on your clipboard to insert into an existing email, document, or OneNote, use the **Copy Link** option.
7	Outlook	If you want to create a new Outlook email because you want to add more content and other attachments, select **Outlook**. Outlook will create a new message with the URL in the body of the email.
8	Send a copy	If you don't want the recipient to have access to the actual file – or, in other words, if you want them to have **a copy** of the file in PDF or native format and not the original – then use the **Send a copy** option. Outlook will create a new email with the file attached formatted either as the native app for the file or as a PDF depending on what you chose.

To configure the permissions (aka Link Settings) before you share with others

This is the important first step!

1. In the top right-hand corner of your document, spreadsheet or presentation, click the **Share** button as seen in Figure 20. This will launch the Sharing window. Alternatively, you can go to the **File** tab and click **Share**.

Figure 20. The Share button in Microsoft Word

2. In the Sharing window under the **Send Link** heading as seen in Figure 21, click the Link Settings arrow to choose the level of access you want to give.

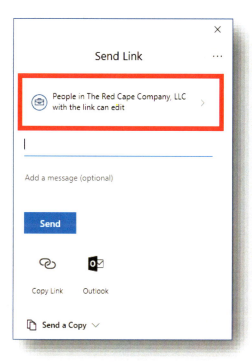

Figure 21. Sharing Window in Word

3. There are four levels of access, as seen in Figure 22 and in the chart. Select the one you need.

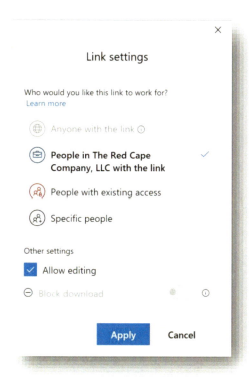

Figure 22. Link settings when sharing files with others

© 2019 Vickie Sokol Evans, MCT; The Red Cape Company, LLC. All Rights Reserved.

Item	Link Settings	Description
1	Anyone with the link	Creates a link that can be shared with anyone, internal or external. (Note: your organization may have disabled this option.)
2	People in [organization name] with the link	Creates a link that can be accessed by anyone in your organization. They must be signed into Office 365 and they must have the link.
3	People with existing access	Creates a link for someone who already has access to the file. Use this when someone needs you to resend the link.
4	Specific people	Creates a link for people you specify either internal or external to your organization. They must have the link and be logged into Office 365. If they forward the link to others, the others will not have access to the file unless you've specifically given them access. (Note: your organization may prevent you from granting access to external recipients.)

4. After you've chosen the appropriate link settings to determine the access level, confirm whether you want to allow editing of the file and/or allow downloading. You're in control! You can always come back and change this later if your colleague needs more access - just repeat steps 1-4.
5. Click **APPLY** to exit link settings.
6. Next, send the link one of three ways:
    - Option A: Send the link (quickly from within the app)
    - Option B: Copy the link (to paste somewhere else)
    - Option C: Send the link to Outlook (to compose a message within Outlook)

Let's dig into these different options at a greater level of detail:

Option A: To send the link to others within the app

If you want to send the link quickly from within Word, Excel, or PowerPoint, use this sending option.

1. First, be sure you've configured the Link Settings as mentioned in the procedure **To configure the permissions (aka Link Settings) before you share with** others beginning on page 30.
2. Then, enter the name and/or email address of the person you want to send it to, as seen in Figure 23.

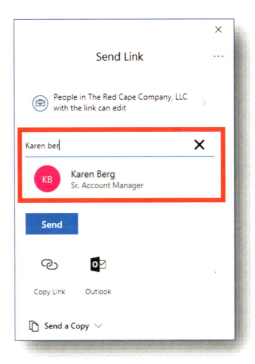

Figure 23. Add the recipient name or email in the Send Link dialog box

3. Add a message, I highly recommend it. In the message area of the Send link dialog box as seen in Figure 23, describe in just a few words or a sentence what the document is and why you're sending it. This helps the recipient if/when they need to search their email for the document later.
4. Click **SEND** to send the document as a link.

Option B: To copy the link to the document

Sometimes you just need to grab the link to the document to paste in an email or in OneNote or other destination.

1. First, be sure you've configured the Link Settings as mentioned in the procedure **To configure the permissions (aka Link Settings) before you share with** others beginning on page 30.
2. Then click **COPY LINK**, as seen in Figure 24, which copies the link to the clipboard.

Figure 24. Copy Link option in the Send Link dialog box

3. Paste wherever you need to paste it.

Option C: To start a new Outlook message, which includes the link

When you need to compose an email message and include other content and perhaps other attachments, use the **OUTLOOK** option when sending the link.

1. First, be sure you've configured the Link Settings as mentioned in the procedure **To configure the permissions (aka Link Settings) before you share with** others beginning on page 30.
2. Then click Outlook, as seen in Figure 25, to launch a new Outlook message with the link automatically pasted in the email. Now you can add written messages, attachments, and anything else you want in the draft email.

Figure 25. The send to Outlook option in the Send Link dialog box

To send a copy or PDF of the file

When you want to share your document but you don't want the recipient to be able to edit the file or collaborate with you in the file, then you'll need to send a copy of the file to them so that they have their own version of the document. In this procedure, we're sending a copy or PDF of a file from within Word, Excel, or PowerPoint.

 You must have Outlook for this to work. If you don't have Outlook, then you can use the old-fashioned way of using the Insert Attachment feature within your email program.

1. In the top right-hand corner of your document, spreadsheet, or presentation, click the **SHARE** button as seen in Figure 20. This will launch the Sharing window.
2. You don't need to configure the Link Settings since you're sending a copy. So, just click **SEND A COPY** and choose between the native file type (Word, Excel, or PowerPoint) or PDF.

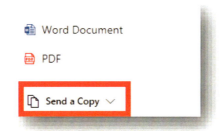

Figure 26. Send a copy of the file

3. Outlook will launch a new message with the file attached.
4. Compose your message and send.

Tip #14   Find a file shared with you (so you don't have to ask for it again!)

Applies to Office 365

When a colleague tells you, "*open the file I shared last week*," and you have NO CLUE what they are talking about or where to find the link, you'll want to master this tip so that you can avoid those embarrassing requests to send it again. Let's look at how to quickly find files that have been shared with you. You can do this in multiple ways:

- From within the Apps (Word, Excel, or PowerPoint) using File > Open > **SHARED WITH ME**
- From within Office 365 Home Page > Recent / Pinned / **SHARED WITH ME** / Discover
- From within Office 365's OneDrive under the heading **SHARED**

© 2019 Vickie Sokol Evans, MCT; The Red Cape Company, LLC. All Rights Reserved.

- From within the OneDrive app on your phone > SHARED

To find shared files from within an App

- From within Word, Excel or PowerPoint, go to the FILE tab, click OPEN, and then click SHARED WITH ME, as seen in Figure 27, and you'll see all the files shared with you by others.

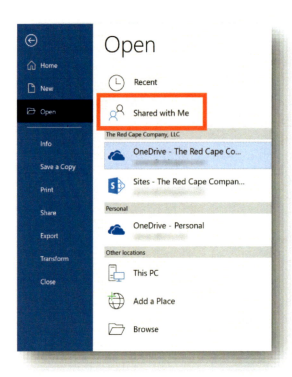

Figure 27. File > Open dialog box in Word showing the Shared with Me option

To find shared files using Office 365's Home Page

1. Log into Office 365 for work or school by going to www.office.com.
2. On the Home page for your account, look below all the apps for the headings: RECENT | PINNED | SHARED WITH ME | DISCOVER, as seen in Figure 28, and click on Shared with me to see all files your colleagues have shared with you.

Figure 28. The Shared with me area on your home page within Office 365

To find shared files using OneDrive online

1. Assuming you're not already in OneDrive online, log into Office 365 for work or school by going to www.office.com.
2. Click the **Apps** launcher button in the top left-hand corner of the **Home** page.

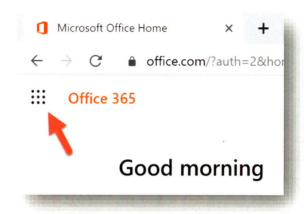

Figure 29. Office 365 Apps Launcher

3. Click the OneDrive app as seen in Figure 30.

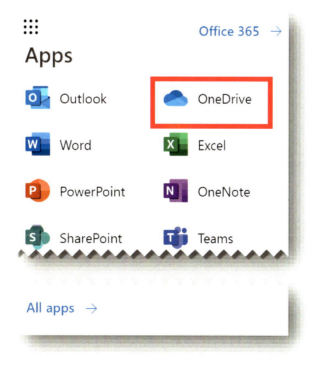

Figure 30. The OneDrive app listed among other Office 365 apps

4. From within OneDrive online, click the Shared category on the left as seen in Figure 31 to see all the files your colleagues have shared with you.

© 2019 Vickie Sokol Evans, MCT; The Red Cape Company, LLC. All Rights Reserved.   37

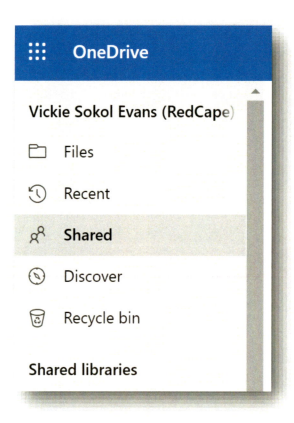

Figure 31. Click Shared within OneDrive online to view files shared with you

To find shared files using the OneDrive app on your smartphone

If you haven't already done so, download the OneDrive app to your smartphone and connect your work/school account.

- To find files shared with you, open OneDrive on your phone and look towards the bottom of the screen for the Shared option, as seen in Figure 32.

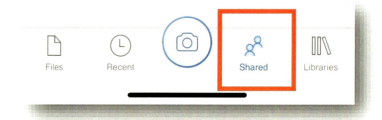

Figure 32. Click Shared within the OneDrive app on your smartphone to view shared files

Tip #15   Edit a document with a colleague at the same time

Applies to Office 365

Now that we've shared a file with our colleague (Tip #13 on page 28) and/or found a file our colleague has shared with us (Tip #14 on page 35), it's time to work together!

As co-authors, we can edit documents from our computer, browser, or smartphone using the respective desktop apps, online apps, or mobile apps for Word, Excel, and PowerPoint. You'll have so much fun working together no matter where you are!

To edit a document at the same time

1. Open the file you want to edit together either in the desktop app, online app, or mobile app. For instance, if you're both editing a Word document, open it in the Word desktop app on your computer, or in Word Online in your browser, or on your smartphone using the Word mobile app.
2. Once you and your colleague(s) are in the file at the same time, you will see the additional authors in the top right-hand corner of the desktop and online apps, as seen in Figure 33. In this example, there is one more person editing the document with me.

Figure 33. Image of the additional editor in this file with me

To see co-authors in the mobile app within the document you're editing, as seen in Figure 34, click the ellipsis (…) to see more options; you'll see "Also Here" as seen in Figure 35.

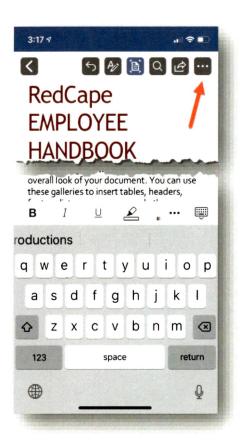

Figure 34. Word mobile app, click the ellipsis (…) to view co-authors

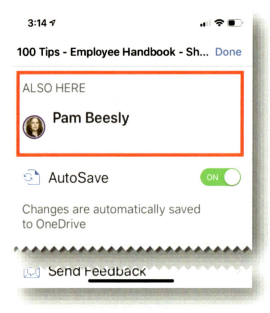

Figure 35. From my mobile phone, I can see who else is editing this document

3. Start editing! You'll see everyone's changes in real time.

 If you don't see real-time changes, there's a chance that you don't have the AutoSave feature turned on. Both the online apps and mobile apps in Office 365 have the AutoSave feature. The desktop app must have AutoSave turned on, as seen in Figure 36. If you don't have AutoSave turned on, then be sure to save regularly so that your co-authors will be able to see your edits and you'll see theirs.

Figure 36. The AutoSave feature

Tip #16 Collaborate with colleagues using interactive comments
Applies to Office 365

Reviewing and editing documents is now easier than ever! We can collaborate using comments within a document, spreadsheet, or presentation with our colleagues.

Once a comment has been added to a sentence in Word, a cell in Excel, or a slide in PowerPoint, other co-authors can add their thoughts to the original comment and then click Resolve when the thread is closed. The main author will then be able to tell that the team has closed the thread and can confidently delete the comment thread when they have all the information they need to proceed.

In this example, we are going to add comments to a presentation.

To reply to comments in a file

1. Click the location on the slide where you want to add a comment or simply click the slide if the comment applies to the entire slide.
2. On the **REVIEW** tab, in the **COMMENTS** group, click **NEW COMMENT** and enter your comment. Alternatively, you can click **COMMENTS** > **NEW COMMENT** in the top right-hand corner of the desktop app or online app. In the mobile app, select the text or location where you want to add a comment and use the mobile menu to add a new comment.

3. Notice that there is a **REPLY** text box underneath your comment as seen in Figure 37. When your colleague sees your comment and wants to respond, he or she can reply directly to the comment so that you know exactly what they are responding to!

Figure 37. Comment thread between Pam and me

4. To modify and delete comments throughout your presentation go to the **REVIEW** tab, in the **COMMENTS** group and use the commands to make your changes. If you have trouble deleting a particular comment, use the **NEXT** and **PREVIOUS** buttons to make the comment active and you will be able to delete it. You can also right-click comments to remove or resolve them.

==This tip meets a MOS certification exam objective.==

Improve your workflow across all programs

Tip #17 Pin your favorite documents to the Open screen
Applies to all versions of Microsoft Office

Like me, you probably have important documents you need regularly, but not necessarily every day. For instance, my team and I store customer testimonials in a document called **RedCape Testimonials**. It's not a document we access every day but it's an important one. So, each member of the team has pinned the document to the Open screen in Word. We've also pinned the **ROI Calculator** Excel file to the Open screen in Excel. It makes it so much easier and efficient to access the files this way instead of having to remember where the documents are saved.

Check out all the Word documents I've pinned for easy access as seen in Figure 38.

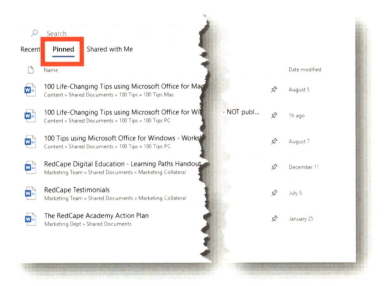

Figure 38. Documents pinned in Microsoft Word

To pin your documents to the Open screen in any Microsoft Office program

1. Open the Word, Excel or PowerPoint file that you want to pin in the desktop app.
2. Click the **FILE** tab and then click **OPEN** to view your recent documents.

© 2019 Vickie Sokol Evans, MCT; The Red Cape Company, LLC. All Rights Reserved.   43

3. Hover over the document you want to pin so that it displays the pin to the right side of the document name and adds a date/time stamp, as seen in Figure 39. If you don't see the document in the Recent list, then open the document so that it shows up in the list.

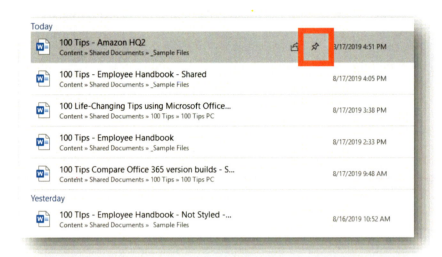

Figure 39. Documents available to pin to the Open screen in Word

4. Click the pin to officially pin it to the list of Pinned documents. The file now will be categorized under the "Pinned" heading.
5. Repeat this for all the important documents you want to quickly gain access to.

Tip #18   Create your own toolbar using the Quick Access Toolbar
Applies to all versions of Microsoft Office

If you like to customize your toolbars, there's good news! You can customize the **Quick Access Toolbar** to display any command you want. The default location for the Quick Access Toolbar is in the top left-hand corner of your Microsoft Office window, above the File and Home tabs as seen in Figure 40. You get three default buttons for each of the Office applications: **Save**, **Undo**, and **Redo**. But let's see how you can easily add more of your favorite commands to your **Quick Access Toolbar**.

Figure 40. Quick Access Toolbar

The Quick Access Toolbar can be positioned either above (by default) or below the ribbon. To move it below the ribbon, right-click the Quick Access Toolbar and choose **SHOW TOOLBAR BELOW THE RIBBON**. To move it back above the Ribbon, right-click the Quick Access toolbar and choose **SHOW TOOLBAR ABOVE THE RIBBON**.

To add a Ribbon command to your Quick Access Toolbar

Do one of the following:

- Click the drop-down arrow to the right of the Quick Access Toolbar and select popular commands to add to the Toolbar, such as **PRINT PREVIEW AND PRINT**, or
- Right-click any command on the Ribbon and choose **ADD TO QUICK ACCESS TOOLBAR**. For example, on the **HOME** tab in the **EDITING** group, right-click **REPLACE** and choose **ADD TO QUICK ACCESS** Toolbar

When a command is no longer a favorite you can remove it by right-clicking the command on the Quick Access Toolbar and choose **REMOVE FROM QUICK ACCESS TOOLBAR**.

To add a command to your Quick Access Toolbar that is NOT in the toolbar list or on the Ribbon

1. Click the drop-down arrow on the right-hand side of the Quick Access Toolbar. Choose from the list of popular commands. Otherwise, click **MORE COMMANDS**.
2. In the **CHOOSE COMMANDS FROM:** list (see item 1 in Figure 41), click the drop-down arrow to select a category of commands. To view all commands alphabetically, choose **ALL COMMANDS** from the drop-down list.

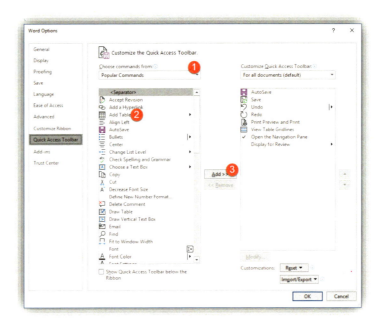

Figure 41. Customize Quick Access Toolbar Window

3. Select the command you want from the list on the left (see item 2 in Figure 41).
4. Click the **ADD >>** button (see item 3 in Figure 41) to add the command to the Quick Access Toolbar list of commands on the right side of the window.
5. Repeat steps 2-4 for each command you wish to add to the Quick Access Toolbar.
6. Click **OK**.

 You can rearrange the commands you added by using the up and down buttons on the right-hand side of the Customize Quick Access Toolbar window in Figure 41. Be sure to highlight the command before you click the move buttons.

 This tip meets a MOS certification exam objective.

Tip #19   Create your own Ribbon

Introduced in Microsoft Office 2010

If you're a power user in any of the Microsoft Office programs, you probably have your favorite go-to commands that make you extremely efficient. Rather

46   © 2019 Vickie Sokol Evans, MCT; The Red Cape Company. All Rights Reserved.

than click between the Ribbon Tabs to get to those commands, you can create your own Ribbon so that they are right at your fingertips.

For instance, I created a new Ribbon Tab to help me write this book more efficiently, as seen in Figure 42. I pulled together all the commands I needed for images, tables, references, and formatting. Plus, I added commands to help me view areas of the document, such as the Navigation pane and page width controls. This dramatically improved my productivity when writing this book!

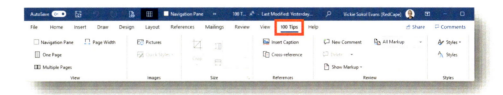

Figure 42. My custom Ribbon in Word

If you want to follow along with this Tip, imagine you are starting any type of large writing project. We are going to create a new Ribbon for that will include five groups of commands in Word, as seen in Figure 42. Note that this is an example for Microsoft Word, but you can do the same thing for Excel and PowerPoint. Get creative! Be more productive.

First, let's examine the Customize Ribbon dialog box.

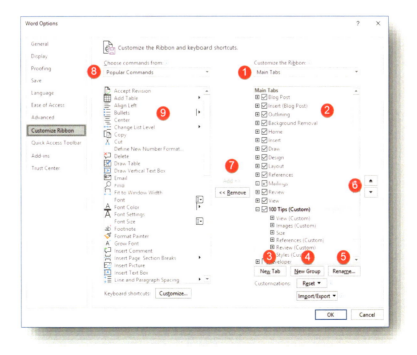

Figure 43. Customize Ribbon dialog box

© 2019 Vickie Sokol Evans, MCT; The Red Cape Company, LLC. All Rights Reserved. 47

	Option	Description
1	**RIBBON TAB CATEGORY** Drop-down	There are three categories of Ribbons: Main Tabs, Tool Tabs, and All Tabs. When creating your own Ribbon, leave it on the default setting of **MAIN TABS**. But feel free to switch between the Tab Categories just to familiarize yourself with the different ones.
2	Ribbon Tab List	The List of Ribbon Tabs based on the Ribbon Tab category selected.
3	**NEW TAB** button	The button to use when you want to create a new Ribbon.
4	**NEW GROUP** button	The button to use to create a new group on your Ribbon.
5	**RENAME** button	The button to use to rename a Ribbon Tab or Group on the Ribbon Tab. You must select the custom Ribbon Tab or the custom Group first before you click the Rename button.
6	**MOVE** buttons	Use the up and down move buttons to move Ribbon Tabs, Groups, or Commands.
7	**ADD AND REMOVE** buttons	Use the Add and Remove buttons to add and remove commands to your custom Ribbon. You can also use the Remove button to get rid of a Ribbon Tab or Group.
8	**COMMAND CATEGORY** Drop-down	Narrow down the list of commands available in the program by using the Command Category.
9	Command List	The List of Commands based on the Command Category selected.

To create your own Ribbon

1. Right-click ANY command on the current Ribbon that is displayed.
2. Choose **CUSTOMIZE THE RIBBON...** to launch the **CUSTOMIZE RIBBON** dialog box seen in Figure 43.
3. The **RIBBON TAB CATEGORY** drop-down (Figure 43, number 1) should be set to **MAIN TABS**; if not, change the category to **MAIN TABS**.

4. We want our new Ribbon Tab to show up after the **View** Tab, so click the **View** Tab in the Main Tab list (Figure 43, option 2).
5. Click the **New Tab** button (Figure 43, option 3) to create a new Ribbon Tab.

Figure 44. Brand new Ribbon Tab and Group before naming them

6. To rename the Ribbon Tab, select **New Tab (Custom)** as seen in Figure 44 and then click the **Rename** button (Figure 43, number 5). Rename it **My Book** or whatever you prefer.
7. Since we need five groups of commands, we need to add four more groups. With the **My Book (Custom)** Ribbon Tab selected, click the **New Group** button four times so that you have five New Groups (Custom) under your new Ribbon Tab, as seen in Figure 45.

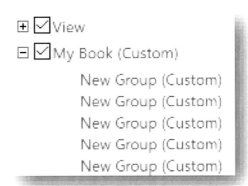

Figure 45. My Book Ribbon Tab with five New Groups (Custom)

8. Let's rename the Groups. Select the first **New Group (Custom)** and click **Rename**. Rename it **View**. Click the next **New Group (Custom)** and click **Rename**. Rename it **Tables**. Repeat for each of the **New Group (Custom)'s** and rename in this order: **Images**, **References**, **Formatting**.
9. Let's add commands to the Ribbon Tab Groups. Select your new **View (Custom)** group.

   The commands we need are on the main **View** Tab. From the **Command Category** drop-down (Figure 43, number 8), choose **Main Tabs** to display all the Main Ribbon Tabs in the Commands list (Figure 43, number 9).

Expand the **View** tab and expand the following two groups: **Show** and **Zoom** as seen in Figure 46.

With the **View (Custom)** Group selected on the right, select **Navigation Pane** on the left under "Show" and click the **Add** button in the middle of the Customize Ribbon dialog box to add the Navigation Pane command to your custom Ribbon Tab. Repeat for **View Whole Page**, **See Multiple Pages**, and **Fit to Window Width**.

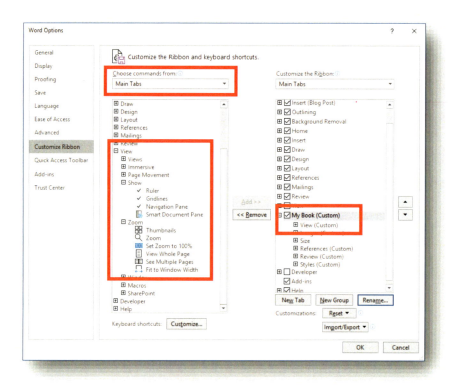

Figure 46. The **View** Ribbon Tab commands in the **Show** and **Zoom** groups

10. Do the same for the remaining commands as described in the table below.

For custom group	To add custom command	Select Command Category	Expand Ribbon Tab > Group > Command
Tables (Custom)	Borders	Tool Tabs	Table Tools > Design Tab > Borders > **Borders**
	View Gridlines	Tool Tabs	Table Tools > Layout Tab > Table > **View Gridlines**
Images (Custom)	Insert Pictures	Main Tabs	Insert Tab > Illustrations > **Insert Picture**

For custom group	To add custom command	Select Command Category	Expand Ribbon Tab > Group > Command
	Quick Styles	Tool Tabs	Picture Tools > Format Tab > Picture Styles > **PICTURE STYLES**
References (Custom)	Insert Caption	Main Tabs	References Tab > Captions > Insert Caption
	Cross-reference	Main Tabs	References Tab > Captions > Cross-Reference
Formatting (Custom)	Styles "Gallery"	Main Tabs	Home Tab > Styles > Text Styles
	Styles "Pane"	Main Tabs	Home Tab > Styles > Text Styles > Styles
	Format Painter	Main Tabs	Home Tab > Clipboard > Format Painter

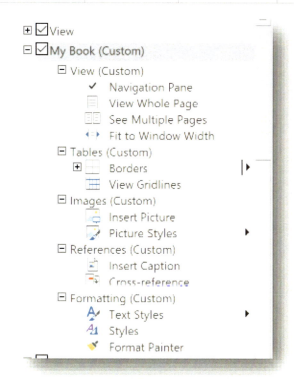

Figure 47. The finished custom Ribbon Tab as seen in the Customize Ribbon dialog box

11. Select **OK** to save.

Custom Ribbons are saved on your computer. If your computer crashes or you get a new one, you will have to rebuild your custom Ribbons on your new device. I recommend that you take a screenshot of your custom Ribbons and save the screenshots in OneNote or a Word document somewhere in a cloud folder so that you have documentation of what you built.

Other Ribbon Options to make you more productive

- **Collapse the Ribbon to show only the tabs** – Double-click any tab OR select **SHOW TABS** from the Ribbon Display Options in the top right-hand corner of your screen, as seen in Figure 48.

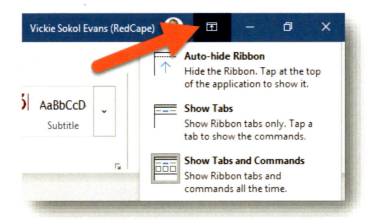

Figure 48. Ribbon Display Options

- **Display the Ribbon to show tabs and commands** – If the Ribbon is hidden, double-click any Ribbon Tab to display the Ribbon OR select **TABS AND COMMANDS** from the Ribbon Display Options in the top right-hand corner of your screen, as seen in Figure 48.
- **To activate shortcut keys (aka Key Tips) for Ribbons and commands** – Press [ALT] on your keyboard (as seen in Figure 49) and then press the corresponding letter for the Ribbon. Keep pressing the letters you see on screen until it launches the command you need.

Figure 49. Key Tips activated

Tip #20 Use the Tell Me feature to get things done faster

Introduced in Office 2016

When you have trouble finding a command in Word, Excel or PowerPoint, don't waste one more second! Use the new TELL ME feature to take you straight to where you want to go.

For instance, if your tables in Microsoft Word don't have borders but you'd like to view the gridlines, type **gridline** in the TELL ME box and Word will present you with a list of possible commands like those seen in Figure 50 within seconds.

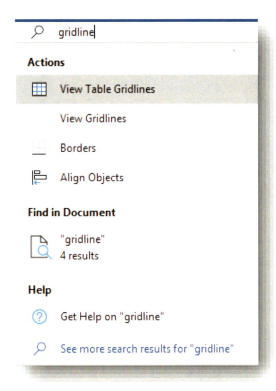

Figure 50. Results from the Tell Me feature in Microsoft Word

If you want to create a PivotTable in Excel, type **pivot** in the TELL ME box to instantly get PivotTable commands, as seen in Figure 51.

© 2019 Vickie Sokol Evans, MCT; The Red Cape Company, LLC. All Rights Reserved.   53

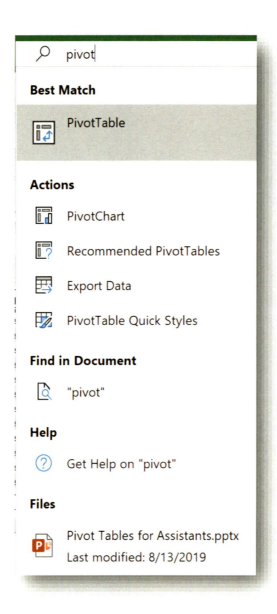

Figure 51. Results from the Tell Me feature in Microsoft Excel

To globally change the font in your PowerPoint presentation, type **fonts** in the TELL ME box and it will present you with the right commands as seen in Figure 52.

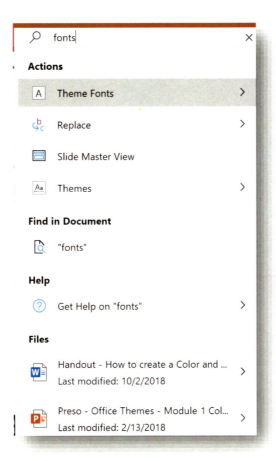

Figure 52. Results from the Tell Me feature in Microsoft PowerPoint

To use Tell Me to get things done faster

1. To the left of your name in the top right-hand corner, click on the magnifying glass seen in Figure 53 or use [ALT]+[Q] to activate the Tell Me feature.

Figure 53. The Tell Me search field in Word

2. Type what you want to do in the simplest terms or the specific command you're looking for and instantly you'll be presented with the commands that you can launch right there without having to go to any Ribbon Tab.

Instantly brand your documents, spreadsheets, and presentations.

Tip #21 Change the color palette for text, tables, and other objects
Introduced in Microsoft Office 2007

It's now exponentially easier to find and change the settings for the default color palette in your documents, spreadsheets, and presentations. This means that your text, graphics and tables will match your corporate brand standards using an expanded list of color options across all Office programs. Doing so not only keeps the Color Police in your office very happy, it also makes your own working life much easier.

Ideally, your marketing department has created and deployed your corporate color set to your ribbon. If they haven't, see steps below on how to create your own Color Set.

To change the color palette of your document

In Microsoft Word

1. Click the **DESIGN** tab in Word.
2. Click the **COLORS** icon in the **DOCUMENT FORMATTING** group to view the color palettes available.
3. Hover over the different Color Sets to preview the look of your document.
4. Click a Color Set to apply it to the document so that it now becomes the default color palette for all objects in the document.

In Microsoft Excel

1. Click the **PAGE LAYOUT** tab in Excel.
2. Click the **COLORS** icon in the **THEMES** group to view the color palettes available.
3. Hover your mouse over the different Color Sets to preview the look of your document.
4. Click the Color Set to apply it to the document's contents.

In Microsoft PowerPoint

1. Click the **DESIGN** tab in PowerPoint.
2. In the **VARIANTS** group, click the **MORE** drop-down button (as seen in Figure 54) and click **COLORS** to view the color palettes available.

Figure 54. Click the More button to reveal Colors palettes for your presentation.

3. Hover your mouse over different color palettes to preview the look of your document.
4. Click the palette to apply it to the document's contents.

In Microsoft Outlook

1. In a new message, click the **Format Text** tab in Outlook.
2. In the **Styles** group, click the **Change Styles** button and click **Colors** to view the color palettes available.
3. Hover your mouse over different color palettes to preview the look of your colors within your email – specifically tables and headings.
4. Click the color palette to apply it to the email and its contents.

 In Office 2010, on the **Page Layout** tab, in the **Themes** group, select the **Colors** button to view the available color palettes.

Create your own Color Set

If the existing options don't meet your needs, you can create your own Color Sets to use throughout your documents, spreadsheets, and presentations. I recommend creating your Color Set in Word. Once you create it in Word, the Color Set will be available to use in Excel, PowerPoint, and Outlook.

1. Create a new document in Word. This ensures you're starting with Word's default template and default color palette, which is configured correctly.
2. On the **Design** tab, in the **Document Formatting** group, click **Colors** and then **Customize Colors** to launch the **Create New Theme Colors** dialog box as seen in Figure 55.

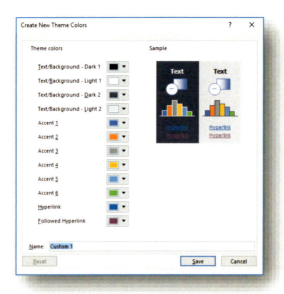

Figure 55. Create New Theme Colors dialog box

3. DO NOT change the first two colors: Dark 1 and Light 1. They should ALWAYS be black and white respectively.
4. I recommend focusing on the 6 accent colors. Click each of them and configure them based on the RGB color setting. If you don't know what the RGB color setting is for your color palette, ask your marketing department.
5. When you're done, give your Color Set a name, such as your company name. For instance, my custom Color Set is "RedCape."
6. Click **SAVE**.
7. You'll be able to use the Color Set in any of the Microsoft Office applications.

This tip meets a MOS certification exam objective.

Tip #22   Globally change the font used in your document
Introduced in Microsoft Office 2007

Experts say you should limit the number of fonts in your document or presentation (and spreadsheet as well) to only two fonts. You should have one font type for your headings and another font for the body text. It's ok to have the same font for both headings and body text but you certainly don't want to have a third font.

The traditional way of changing fonts is to select all your text in your document and use the Font drop-down box to switch to a new font. The new and improved way is to set the font at the Theme level so that the font is changed within the entire document and flows downstream throughout your document.

Themes are explained in detail in Tip #22. Meanwhile, here's the correct way to globally change your font.

To globally change the font in your document

In Microsoft Word

1. Without selecting anything, go to the **DESIGN** tab, in the **DOCUMENT FORMATTING** group, click the arrow for **FONTS**.
2. Choose one of the Font Sets or create your own font set (as outlined below).

In Microsoft Excel

1. Without selecting anything, go to the **PAGE LAYOUT** tab, in the **THEMES** group, click the arrow for **FONTS**.
2. Choose one of the Font Sets or create your own font set (as outlined below).

In Microsoft PowerPoint

1. On the **DESIGN** tab, in the **VARIANTS** group, click the drop-down arrow and select **FONTS**.
2. Select the font set you want; this will update the Slide Master and its layouts with the correct heading and body fonts.

In Microsoft Outlook

1. Click the **FORMAT TEXT** tab in Outlook.
2. In the **STYLES** group, click the **CHANGE STYLES** button and click **FONTS** to view the color palettes available.
3. Hover your hover over different fonts to preview the look of your email.
4. Click the Font set to apply it to the email and its contents.

Create your own Font Set

If the standard list of Font Sets described in the previous tip don't meet your needs, you can create your own to use throughout your documents, spreadsheets and presentations.

© 2019 Vickie Sokol Evans, MCT; The Red Cape Company, LLC. All Rights Reserved.

- Using the Font Set drop-down (see steps above) click **CUSTOMIZE FONTS** and identify the font for your Headings and Body Text, then give your Font Set a name such as the name of your company, such as **ABC Company**.

Set your favorite Font Set as the default for your documents

If you grow tired of selecting the Font Set every time you create or manage a document, you can set your favorite font set as the default.

1. Make sure the Font Set exists by either finding it in the list of Font Sets or creating a new font set as explained in the procedure above.
2. Go ahead and select the Font Set for the document to be the default for new documents.

In Microsoft Word

- On the **DESIGN** tab, in the **DOCUMENT FORMATTING** group, click **SET AS DEFAULT**. When you create a new Word document, the new fonts will now be the default for that document and any document moving forward. It will not affect existing documents.

In Microsoft Excel

- You'll have to save the blank file with the default font and color set as a template.

In Microsoft PowerPoint

- You'll have to set up your Slide Master using a Theme to save the font and colors as defaults. More about this in Chapter 5. See Tip #66.

This tip meets a MOS certification exam objective.

Tip #23 Brand your documents using Themes

Introduced in Microsoft Office 2007

In the previous two tips, you learned how to set the global colors and fonts in your documents. To save even more time, you can use a Theme, which combines both the Color Set and Font Set together for one-click application to your deliverable. A Theme also includes graphic Effects for charts and objects as well as options for Layouts, Backgrounds, and Slide Masters in PowerPoint.

With a Theme, you're one-click away from creating consistent, professional-looking, and branded deliverables, PLUS you'll be able to re-purpose and share content seamlessly between Word, Excel, & PowerPoint.

To change your document theme

In Microsoft Word

1. On the **DESIGN** tab, at the beginning of the **DOCUMENT FORMATTING** group, select the **THEMES** button to view the available Office themes.
2. Click to select the one you want to apply.

In Microsoft Excel

1. Go to the **PAGE LAYOUT** tab, in the **THEMES** group, click the arrow for **THEMES**.
2. Choose one of the Themes to apply to your spreadsheet

In Microsoft PowerPoint

- On the **DESIGN** tab, in the **THEMES** group, select one of the Themes available to you.

Creating your own Theme. A Theme is an incredible timesaving feature of Office that provides consistent branding across all Office with one click of a button. The proper way to create your own Theme is in PowerPoint because Themes in PowerPoint include many more elements. Once you have a company Theme created in PowerPoint, all the other programs can use that Theme. See chapter 5 for more information.

Contact RedCape if you are interested in creating corporate themes for your company or clients. www.redcapeco.com/contact-us. Or visit www.redcapeco.com/themes to see the timesaving benefits of a Theme.

In Office 2010, on the **PAGE LAYOUT** tab, in the **THEMES** group, select the **THEMES** button to view the available Office themes

This tip meets a MOS certification exam objective.

Manage your file behind the scenes.

Tip #24   Create, email, and convert PDFs

Introduced in Microsoft Office 2007

Woohoo! No more third-party tools needed to save your Office document to a PDF. Since Office 2007, you can save any Word, Excel or PowerPoint file as a PDF and my ultimate favorite…instead of saving a file as a PDF, you can email a file as a PDF, which allows you to bypass the saving process and eliminate all of those random PDF files you have on your hard drive or network drive.

I bet you're wondering, "Yeah, but can you convert a PDF back into a document?"

Yes! This capability was introduced in Office 2013!

You asked. Microsoft delivered. New in Office 2013 is the ability to convert your PDF back into a Word document so that you can edit a PDF in Word.

Save a file as PDF using Save As

1. In any file, on the **FILE** tab, click **SAVE AS**.
2. In the **SAVE AS TYPE** drop-down, select **PDF**.

Save a file as PDF using Export

1. In any file, on the **FILE** tab, click **EXPORT**.
2. Click **CREATE PDF/XPS DOCUMENT** as seen in Figure 56.

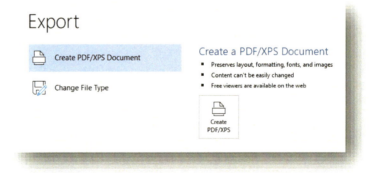

Figure 56. Backstage Window – Create a PDF using Export

 To save a file as a PDF in previous versions, click the Office button and choose SAVE AS. Then click PDF OR XPS.

Email a file as a PDF

Applies to all versions of Microsoft Office

Since Office 2007, we could now save our documents in PDF format without needing a third-party tool. But the challenge with creating so many PDFs is that now we're keeping track of two "file types" for the one document: one in its original format (docx, xlsx, pptx) and the second one as a PDF. Hmm - that just won't do. If you need to email a copy of your file to someone as a PDF, you can simply email the file as a PDF and bypass the save step altogether.

We saw this in Tip #13 "Share files with others effortlessly " on page 28. But I want to include the steps if you are using a previous version of Microsoft Office.

To email a document as a PDF in previous versions of Office

1. On the FILE tab, click SHARE.
2. Click EMAIL as seen in Figure 56, then click SEND AS PDF.

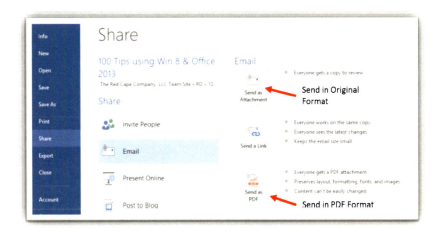

Figure 57. Backstage Window: Email as a PDF

 To email a document as a PDF in Office 2010, click FILE, then SAVE AND SEND. Then click SEND USING EMAIL, then click SEND AS PDF.

This tip meets a MOS certification exam objective.

Convert a PDF to a Word document

It's finally here! You can now convert a PDF to Word.

Introduced in Microsoft Word 2013

1. In Word, from the **FILE** tab, click **OPEN**.
2. Navigate to your PDF file.
3. Select the PDF file and click **OPEN**.
4. Click **OK** if you get the "This may take a while" message.
5. Make changes to the file.
6. To save back to a PDF, from the **FILE** tab, click **SAVE AS**.
7. Once you find the location where you want to save the document, be sure to select **PDF** from the **SAVE AS TYPE**, otherwise Word will want to save it as a Word document by default.

This tip meets a MOS certification exam objective.

Tip #25   Remove personal data (aka Metadata)

Applies to all versions of Microsoft Office

Before you share you document with others, you may want to remove personal data contained in the document such as the author's name (which may or may not be you), editing time, customer information, etc., especially if it isn't accurate. This personal data is called "metadata" and is required in all files because it helps your computer index and find files quickly during a search. In this tip, we'll see how to view and erase metadata.

Additionally, you can remove other types of elements such as comments, track changes, and hidden content. Here is a full list of the types of things you can inspect for and remove instantly from your documents, spreadsheets and presentations.

INSPECT FOR AND REMOVE	WORD	EXCEL	POWERPOINT
Comments, Revisions, Versions, Annotations	X	X	X
Document Properties and Personal Information	X	X	X
Task Pane Apps	X	X	X
Content Apps		X	X
Collapsed Headings	X		
Custom XLM Data	X	X	X
Headers, Footers	X	X	
Watermarks	X		
Invisible Content	X	X	
Invisible On-Slide Content			X
Off-Slide Content			X
Hidden Text	X		
Hidden Rows and Columns		X	
Hidden Worksheets			
Data Model			

First, let's begin by reviewing the metadata contained in the document's properties and then walk through the steps to instantly erase that data before sending it to a customer or potential employer, or adversary.

To view personal data

1. Click the **FILE** tab to launch Backstage view. By default, this displays the **INFO** section.
2. On the right side of the **INFO** SECTION is a list of properties about the document (as seen in Figure 58). This is the document's metadata.
3. To view more properties, click the **SHOW ALL PROPERTIES** link at the bottom of the list of properties.

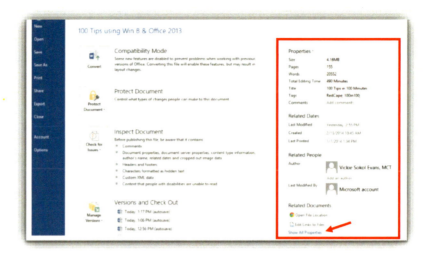

Figure 58. Backstage View: document properties

To avoid the risk of sharing personal or private document information (which may or may not be accurate), you may want to remove the metadata from the file before sending the document to someone.

To remove your personal data

1. Click the **File** tab to get Backstage again and to display the **Info** section.
2. Click the **Check for Issues** button in the middle of the **Backstage** view and choose **Inspect Document** to launch the Document Inspector as seen in Figure 59.
3. Click **Inspect** to view all the metadata found in the document.
4. Click **Remove All** for **Document Properties and Personal Info**.

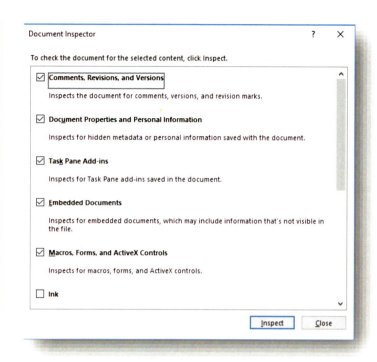

Figure 59. Document Inspector for Word

This tip meets a MOS certification exam objective.

Chapter 3: Microsoft Word Tips

Save time, effectively present your information, eliminate problematic formatting, and deliver a professional document that will crush the competition.

In this Chapter

- Use timesaving shortcuts to improve your writing time and decrease formatting time
- Organize content with minimal effort and maximum confidence
- Format short and long documents with 100% consistency
- Discover ways to convert your document into different formats and structures
- Format your documents in *minutes*, not hours
- Navigate confidently throughout your document

Save hours of formatting time.

Tip #26 Discover selecting tricks using the document margin

Applies to all versions of Microsoft Word

What happens when you move your mouse to the left margin in your document? Did it turn into a white arrow pointing to the right as in Figure 60? The arrow shape actually has a purpose, believe it or not. The purpose of this arrow is to quickly select text with precision.

Figure 60. Selection arrow

To use the selection arrow

1. Move your mouse to the left-hand margin next to the text you wish to select.
2. Then perform the following actions:

Selection Arrow	Action
Single-click	Selects one line of text
Double-click	Selects one paragraph
Triple-click	Selects entire document

Tip #27   Use Styles to format your document

Applies to all versions of Microsoft Word

When working in long documents or repeatedly in short documents, you can save yourself considerable amount of time by using styles. Styles are saved sets of formatting instructions you can apply to a selection or entire paragraph. Not only do Styles save you formatting time, but they also create a consistent and branded look for your document and makes updating the document a breeze. Styles also reduce formatting errors, which can prevent hours of troubleshooting (and stress) later.

To apply a Title style

1. Click in the paragraph that contains the title of the document.
2. On the **HOME** tab, in the **STYLES** group, click the style called **TITLE** as seen in Figure 61.

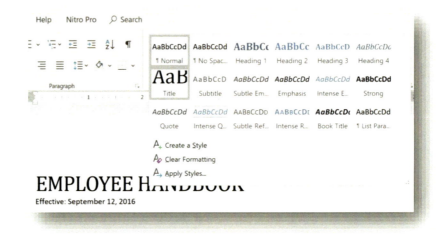

Figure 61. Apply the Title Style to the title of the document.

Note: If you do not see the Title style in the Styles gallery, click the **More** button on the side of the Styles window to display more styles as seen in Figure 62.

Figure 62. Styles Gallery "More" button

To apply styles to your headings

1. Click in one of your main heading paragraphs.
2. On the **Home** tab, in the **Styles** group, click the Quick Style called **Heading 1**.
3. If this main heading has a subheading, click in the first subheading.
4. On the **Home** tab, in the **Styles** group, click the Quick Style called **Heading 2**.
5. Repeat as necessary, using the Headings 1-9 to establish your document hierarchy.

Your heading levels correspond with the hierarchy of your document headings, sub-headings, sub sub-headings and so on – similar to an outline.

This tip meets a MOS certification exam objective.

Tip #28   Use F4 to repeat last action

Applies to all versions of Microsoft Word

When you need to repeat the very last action in Word, you can use the keyboard shortcut [F4]. For instance, in the previous tip, you applied Heading 2 style to one of your sub-headings. If you want to continue applying Heading 2 for the remainder of your level 2 headings in your document, you can scroll through your document and use the [F4] keyboard shortcut to apply the Heading 2 style.

To repeat the last action

1. After making a change to text, such as applying a heading style, navigate to the next heading that needs the same style you just applied.
2. Press [F4] to repeat the last action, which was applying your heading.
3. Navigate to the next heading that needs the same style and press [F4].
4. Repeat for the remainder of the document.

[F4] only repeats the very last action. For example, if you applied a heading style, and then deleted some text in a paragraph below it, only the delete action would repeat, as this was the last action take.

Alternative shortcut. [F4] is the same thing as using [Ctrl]+[Y] in other programs like Excel, PowerPoint and Outlook. However, Word is the only application where you can use either [F4] or [Ctrl]+[Y].

Tip #29   Select all text with similar formatting

Applies to all versions of Microsoft Word

When working in long documents or documents with a variety of formatting that must be consistent, such as a resume, you need a way to select all similarly formatted text throughout the entire document. Use the timesaving feature SELECT ALL TEXT WITH SIMILAR FORMATTING so that you can effortlessly

- format the selected text a different way,
- copy and paste the content to another location or to another document, or
- delete content.

To select all text with similar formatting and apply a Style

1. Click in the paragraph you want to use as your sample paragraph.
2. On the **HOME** tab, in the **EDITING** group, click **SELECT** to launch the Select menu as seen in Figure 63.
3. Click **SELECT ALL TEXT WITH SIMILAR FORMATTING**.
4. Apply the appropriate style to the selected text in your document.

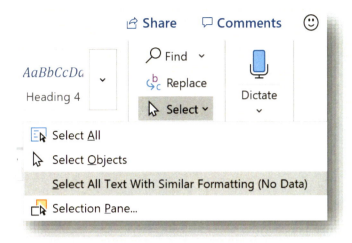

Figure 63. Select All Text With Similar Formatting (No Data)

To select all text with similar formatting to paste into another document or to delete

1. Click in one of the paragraphs you wish to copy or delete.
2. On the **Home** tab, in the **Editing** group, click **Select** to launch the Select menu as seen in Figure 63.
3. Click **Select All Text With Similar Formatting**.
4. Copy the selection and paste into another document; or, if you want to delete the text, simply delete the selection.

Tip #30   Reformat your document in seconds using Style Sets
Introduced in Word 2007

> When you apply the standard Title and Heading styles to your document, your document takes on the format of the default Styles in Word. If you don't like the way your document looks after you've styled it, never fear! Style Sets are here!!
>
> Style Sets are a collection of styles that can be used to instantly change the look of your document so that you're using the best format for that document type. For instance, resumes look different from travel Itineraries, which look different from Proposals. Each of these document types would represent a different Style Set that you could create and save for reuse.
>
> In the previous example, we styled our document using the default Title and Headings. Now let's completely restructure the document by changing the Style Set.

To use a Style Set to restructure your document

1. Click the **DESIGN** tab.
2. Hover over any of the Style Sets in the Style Set gallery to preview the changes to the document. Once you find one that works, simply click to choose it.

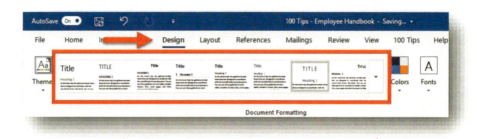

Figure 64. Change Style Set

In Office 2010, on the **HOME** tab, in the **STYLES** group, click the **CHANGE STYLES** button.

This tip meets a MOS certification exam objective.

Tip #31 Modify a style

Applies to all versions of Microsoft Word

One of the many ways to modify a style is to right-click the style name and select the option to modify it. This is called "modify by definition."

To modify a style by definition

1. On the **HOME** tab, in the **STYLES** group, right-click the style you wish to modify in the Quick Styles gallery.
2. Choose **MODIFY…** to open the Modify Style dialog box as seen in Figure 65.
3. Use the tools in the Formatting section of the dialog box to edit the style or click the **FORMAT** drop-down button at the bottom left-hand corner of the dialog box to see more formatting options.

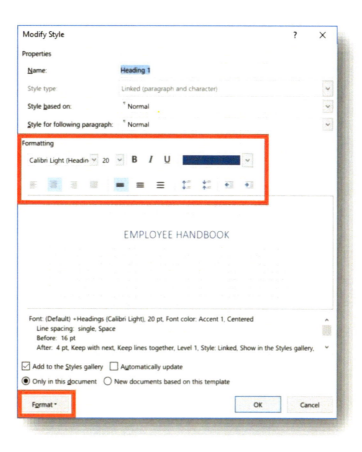

Figure 65. Modify Style dialog box

 This tip meets a MOS certification exam objective.

Tip #32   Create a table of contents in seconds
Applies to all versions of Microsoft Word

There are a couple of ways you can create a table of contents (also known as a "TOC"): you can either mark entries in your document that you want displayed in your TOC, or you can tell Word to generate the TOC from your styles.

Since you've already styled your document (see Tip #27), the easiest way to create a table of contents is from your heading styles. The procedure below assumes you formatted a document using heading styles.

Create a table of contents from your heading styles

1. Click where you want to insert the table of contents, usually TOCs are at the beginning of a document.
2. On the **REFERENCES** tab, in the **TABLE OF CONTENTS** group, click **TABLE OF CONTENTS**, and then click the Automatic Table 1 style or the Automatic Table 2 style as seen in Figure 66.

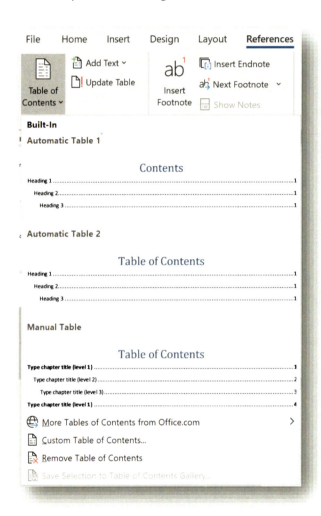

Figure 66. Table of Contents menu on the ribbon

To customize your Table of Contents

1. Click somewhere in your TOC.
2. Click the **REFERENCES** tab.
3. In the **TABLE OF CONTENTS** group, click the **TABLE OF CONTENTS** drop-down arrow and choose **CUSTOMIZE TABLE OF CONTENTS** to open the Table of Contents window.

Figure 67. Table of Contents window

4. Configure the settings for your TOC. I encourage you to test the different options for creating a TOC that works for your document. Meanwhile, here are some suggested settings:
   - Show page number (ON by default)
   - Right align page numbers (ON by default)
   - Tab leader (set to dotted tab leader by default)
   - Formats (choose your favorite)
   - Show Levels (set how many heading levels you want)
   - Options – select the Options button if you need to select additional styles to bring into your TOC
5. Click **OK**.

In Word 2010 and earlier, on the **REFERENCES** tab, in the **TABLE OF CONTENTS** group, click **INSERT TABLE OF CONTENTS** to launch the Table of Contents window.

This tip meets a MOS certification exam objective.

© 2019 Vickie Sokol Evans, MCT; The Red Cape Company, LLC. All Rights Reserved.   77

Tip #33   Create a professional cover page in an instant

Introduced in Word 2007

When creating a title page or cover page for your document, you can eliminate the time-consuming process of inserting a blank page, adding your title, subtitle, company info, lots of blank lines to position the content, and section breaks to control the page numbering. You can even eliminate the time it takes to format all the various elements of your cover page. You can do this by inserting one of Word's professionally designed cover pages.

Create a professional cover page in an instant

1. You don't have to worry about where your cursor is since Cover Pages are always added to the beginning of your document. On the **INSERT** tab, in the **PAGES** group, click the **COVER PAGE** drop-down.
2. Scroll through the gallery of cover pages to select the one you want. Word will insert your new cover page at the beginning of the document.
3. Using the document controls to guide you, enter the applicable Title, Subtitle, Author, etc. in the cover page.
4. To change to a different cover page, repeat steps 1 and 2 above. There is no need to remove the original cover page.

This tip meets a MOS certification exam objective.

Work like a pro.

Tip #34   Add letters from a foreign alphabet
Applies to all versions of Microsoft Word

In the olden days, aka 'the 1900's", aka "the 90's", it was geeky cool to memorize a handful of ALT codes to insert foreign characters, such as [Alt]+164 for the ñ character and [Alt]+0225 for an á. But there is a much easier way to insert foreign characters that requires only one thing to memorize. This is sure to impress anyone in your office and make you more "cool" and less geeky.

How to add letters from a foreign alphabet

- When you come to a letter that needs an accent, before you type that letter, hold down [Ctrl] and type the accent (such as ' or ^ or ~), then immediately type the letter that will go under the symbol.

    For example, to type "Réne", first type the **R** and then type [CTRL]+ the apostrophe ['], let go of [CTRL] and then immediately type **ene**.

    To type "piñata", first type the **pi** and then type [CTRL]+[SHIFT]+the tilde symbol [~], let go of [CTRL]+[SHIFT] and then immediately type **nata**. We had to include [Shift] this time because the tilde symbol [~] is on the top row of the keyboard buttons.

    Note: If you want to see the table of special [Alt] characters search the Web for **Alt Codes**. There are numerous sites with the full list of codes and instructions on how to use them.

Tip #35   Find and replace special characters
Applies to all versions of Microsoft Word

Sometimes when you copy content from an email or from the Web and paste it into Word, the text doesn't wrap naturally. When you turn on your paragraph marks using the Show/Hide command, you'll discover that there are manual line breaks forcing the content to prematurely move to the next line. You can use the find and replace feature to find all instances of the manual line break and replace with a space.

To replace manual line breaks with a space

1. To view line breaks, turn on your paragraph marks. On the **HOME** tab, in the **PARAGRAPH** group, click the **SHOW/HIDE** button as seen in Figure 68.

Figure 68. The Show/Hide paragraph marks command on the Home ribbon

2. Now that you can see where the line breaks are, select the content you want to remove line breaks from.
3. On the **HOME** tab in the **EDITING** group, click **REPLACE**.
4. Click in the **FIND WHAT** field and clear out anything left over from a previous Find.
5. Click the **MORE** button seen in Figure 69 to expand your Find and Replace window to reveal more options as seen in Figure 70. Note: if you see the **LESS** button, your window is already expanded.

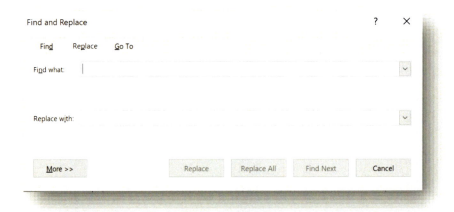

Figure 69. The More button in the Find and Replace dialog box

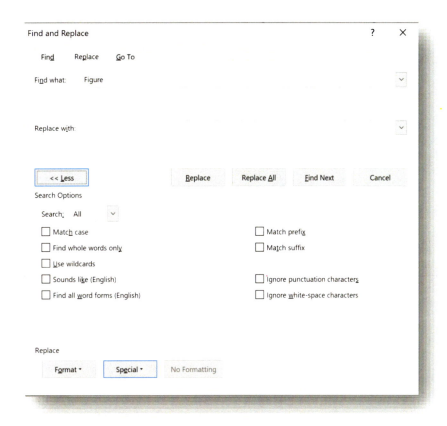

Figure 70. Find and Replace More Dialog Box

6. Click the **Special** button and choose **Manual Line Break**. This places a special code in the **Find What** field.
7. Click in the **Replace With** field and clear out anything left over from a previous Replace.
8. In the **Replace With** field press the spacebar once, which places a space in that field.
9. Click **Replace All** and then click **No** when asked if you want to search the remaining document.

To replace semicolons and a space with carriage returns

Another example is when you need to convert a list of email addresses copied from an email "To:" field to a list of emails that are on separate lines. This is helpful when you plan to paste the emails in Excel or need to import the emails into a database.

1. It's always good to turn on your paragraph marks to see what's happening with the spaces, line breaks, and carriage returns. On the **Home** tab, in the

Paragraph group, click the **Show/Hide** button so you can see exactly what's between each email.
2. Select the content you want to affect. This isn't necessary if you want to make the change to the entire document.
3. On the **Home** tab in the **Editing** group, click **Replace**.
4. Click in the **Find What** field and clear out anything left over from a previous Find.
5. Type a semi-colon [;] and a space in the **Find What** field.
6. Click the **More** button to expand your Find and Replace window to reveal more options. Note: if you see the **Less** button, your window is already expanded.
7. Click in the **Replace With** field and clear out anything left over from a previous Replace.
8. Click the **Special** button and choose **Paragraph Mark**. This places a special code in the **Replace With** field.
9. Click **Replace All** and then click **No** when asked if you want to search the remaining document.

==This tip meets a MOS certification exam objective.==

Effortlessly design and manage tables

Tip #36   Format a table in seconds

Applies to all versions of Microsoft Word

Not only can you instantly format text using styles, you can do the same for your tables using Table styles. When you click inside a table, you will see the Table Tools contextual tabs appear on the Ribbon as seen in Figure 71. If you do not see these tabs, you have not clicked inside a table.

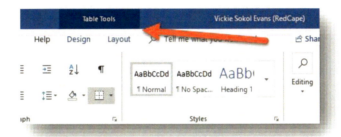

Figure 71. Table Tools contextual tabs on the Ribbon

To format your table using a table style

1. Click in your table or select it so that you see the Table Tools contextual tabs on the ribbon.
2. On the **TABLE TOOLS DESIGN** tab, in the **TABLE STYLES** group, click the **MORE** button to expand the list of Table Styles, as seen in Figure 72.

Figure 72. The Table Styles "More" button on the Table Design ribbon

3. Hover over any of the sample styles to see what it will look like in your document.
4. Click the style you wish to apply.

This tip meets a MOS certification exam objective.

Tip #37 Effortlessly move table rows

Applies to all versions of Microsoft Word

Your table looks amazing (after Tip #36) but you notice a slight problem. You realize that you need to move content from one row, above another row. Rather than insert a row and retype the info, you can use a powerful keyboard shortcut.

To effortlessly move table rows

1. Click in the row that needs to be moved.
2. Press [Shift]+[Alt]+Up Arrow (or Down Arrow) to move the row to the right spot.

Tip #38 Confidently delete a table

Applies to all versions of Microsoft Word

When you want to delete your table, it is common to select the entire table and then press the [DELETE] key on your keyboard. Unfortunately, that deletes only the text.

To delete the entire table, including the text

- Select the table and use the [BACKSPACE] key instead of the [DELETE] key.

Navigate quickly throughout your document.

Tip #39 Use your headings and keyboard shortcuts to navigate your document

Applies to all versions of Microsoft Word

Once you have styles applied to your headings and subheadings, you can use those headings to navigate quickly through your document by using Word's Navigation Pane.

To use the Navigation Pane to navigate your document

1. On the **VIEW** tab, in the **SHOW** group, click the **NAVIGATION PANE** check box. If you are using Styles for your headings, hooray! You will see your headings and subheadings in the Navigation Pane on the left side of your screen.
2. Click on any heading text in the Navigation Pane to jump to that section in the document.

Note: If you do not see anything in the Navigation Pane after Step #1 above, that means the document isn't formatted using Heading styles. Go back to Tip #27 and apply your Heading styles to your main headings and subheadings.

Use keyboard shortcuts to navigate your document

Applies to all versions of Microsoft Word

Use these universal keyboard shortcuts to help you get around you document faster than ever before! All four of these shortcuts apply to most Microsoft Office programs as well as other technologies.

To go to the top of your document

- Use the [CTRL]+[HOME] keyboard shortcut.

To go to the end of your document

- Use the [CTRL]+[END] keyboard shortcut.

To go to the beginning of a line

- Use the [HOME] keyboard shortcut.

To go to the end of the line

- Use the [END] keyboard shortcut.

This tip meets a MOS certification exam objective.

Tip #40   Easily move content like never before

Introduced in Word 2010

It is now easier than ever to move blocks of content to another location in your document by using the Navigation Pane. This is a great way to change the order of content within your document rather than using cut-and-paste or drag and drop, both of which can be risky. When you move headings in your navigation pane, the corresponding subheadings (if any) and body text, tables, and other objects will move with it.

To move content using the Navigation Pane

1. Display your Navigation Pane. On the **View** tab in the **Show** group, click the **Navigation Pane** check box. If you are using Styles for your headings and text, hooray! You will see your headings and subheadings in the Navigation Pane on the left side of your screen.
2. In the Navigation Pane, drag the heading you want to move above or below another heading in the document.

As seen in Figure 73, you can also right-click any heading to perform additional actions such as:

- Promoting or demoting a heading
- Adding a new heading before or after the current heading
- Adding a subheading
- Deleting a heading
- Selecting Heading and Content
- Printing heading and content
- Expanding and collapse headings
- Specifying which heading levels to view

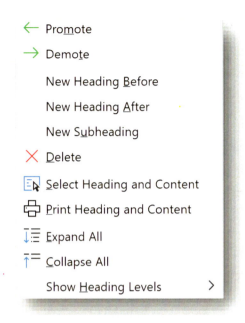

Figure 73. Navigation Pane Right-Click Menu

 Note: If you do not see anything in the Navigation Pane after Step #1 above, that means the document isn't formatted using styles. Go back to Tip #27.

 This tip meets a MOS certification exam objective.

© 2019 Vickie Sokol Evans, MCT; The Red Cape Company, LLC. All Rights Reserved.

Chapter 4: Microsoft Excel Tips

Save time, improve accuracy, eliminate errors, effectively present your data, and make better business decisions.

In this Chapter

- Use timesaving shortcuts to improve efficiency and accuracy
- Organize and understand data with minimal effort and confidence using Tables
- Discover ways to fix problems with your data and reduce errors
- Find and make sense of your data to analyze trends

Save time using "back to basics" tools.

Tip #41 Discover Autofill tips to save data entry time and prevent mistakes

Applies to all versions of Microsoft Excel

When working with time dimensions such as days, weeks, months, quarters and time of day, you can count on Excel to do much of the work for you when it comes to typing the data into your sheet. After typing one month or day of the week, use a feature called Autofill to fill in the pattern and complete the list. For instance, suppose you need the months "Jan" through "Dec" across your sheet as column headers; to do this, just type the first month and then use Autofill to complete the remaining months.

© 2019 Vickie Sokol Evans, MCT; The Red Cape Company, LLC. All Rights Reserved.   89

Examples of series that you can fill

Start with...	Use Autofill to complete the series...
Jan	Feb, Mar, Apr,...
Jan, Apr	Jul, Oct, Jan,...
Jan-07, Apr-07	Jul-07, Oct-07, Jan-08,...
15-Jan, 15-Apr	15-Jul, 15-Oct,...
2007, 2008	2009, 2010, 2011,...
1-Jan, 1-Mar	1-May, 1-Jul, 1-Sep,...
Qtr3 (or Q3 or Quarter3)	Qtr4, Qtr1, Qtr2,...
1, 2, 3	4, 5, 6,...
9:00	10:00, 11:00, 12:00,...
Mon	Tue, Wed, Thu,...
Monday	Tuesday, Wednesday, Thursday,...
text1, textA	text2, textA, text3, textA,...
1st Period	2nd Period, 3rd Period,...
Product 1	Product 2, Product 3,...

To Autofill months in your sheet

1. Type the name of the first month in a cell. Type either the full month or the abbreviated 3-character version, such as "Jan." for January, and press [ENTER].

2. Hover your mouse over the AutoFill handle located in the bottom right-hand corner of your selected cell as seen in Figure 74. Your mouse pointer will turn into a black plus sign.

	Jan		
Catalog	35220	26162	31809
Online	51007	66193	69480
Reseller	38512	47688	50372
Store	162066	267533	229591

Figure 74. Drag the Fill handle on the cell to autofill the series.

3. Drag the black plus sign either down or to the right to Autofill the remaining values.

Create a schedule in 30-minute increments

Autofill also works with date and time, but there's one extra little step when working with dates and time because Excel doesn't know what increment you want. If you Autofill a date, such as today's date, Excel will assume you want the next value to be one day later and the series will Autofill by increments of a day. But what if you wanted to increase by weeks or months instead of days?

Likewise, when you Autofill a time, such as 8:00 AM, Excel gives you the next hour, 9:00AM. But what if you wanted 30 minute increments instead of hour increments? The trick is to tell Excel exactly what you want by typing in the first two values and THEN Autofill both of those values to complete the series.

To create a schedule in 30-minute increments

1. For example, in the first cell, type **8:00 AM**, press [Return].
2. In the second cell, type **8:30 AM**, press [Return].
3. Select both cells as seen in Figure 75.

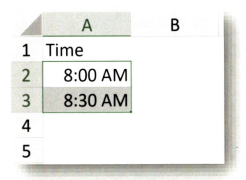

Figure 75. AutoFill Time using a specific increment

4. Hover over the Autofill handle located in the bottom right-hand corner of the second cell – the **8:30 AM** cell – until your mouse turns into the shape of a small, black plus sign.
5. Drag down as needed.

Copy calculations using autofill

Not only can you use Autofill to increment time dimensions as we saw in the previous steps, but you can also use it to copy calculations.

As seen in the table below, the Total for January sales has been calculated and is selected. Rather than type the calculation in each of the other locations or copy and paste the calculation, you can instead use Autofill to save even more time.

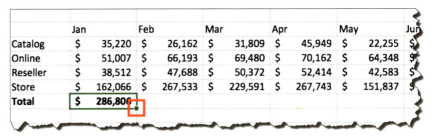

Figure 76. Use the Fill handle to copy calculations.

1. Create the calculation in the first Total cell of your series by using the SUM() function. In my example I typed, **=Sum(B3:B6)**, where B3 is the cell address for the first value ($35,220) and B6 is the cell address for the last value ($162,066) in the range of data.
2. Use the Autofill handle located in the bottom right-hand corner of your selected "Total" cell to drag to the right across the columns.

To instantly autofill down a column

Now that you have had a little practice using Autofill to enter time dimensions in different increments and to copy calculations, it is time to learn yet another timesaving shortcut using Autofill. Rather than drag the Autofill handle, you can double-click the Autofill handle to automatically fill the series for you.

1. Select the cell you wish to Autofill down your list of data.
2. Position your mouse pointer on the Autofill handle (the bottom right-hand corner of the cell).
3. When your mouse pointer turns into a black plus sign, **double-click** the Autofill handle and the data is instantly added down the column.

This trick only works for filling data down a column. It does not work for data across rows. Additionally, for the Autofill handle to copy instantly down the column, there must be a data column to the left or right; otherwise the double-click option will not work and you will need to drag the mouse down instead.

If the Autofill handle finds a cell that is already filled with data, it will NOT overwrite what is already in that cell, and it will stop as soon as it comes to a cell with data in it.

This tip meets a MOS certification exam objective.

Tip #42   Quickly select your data

Applies to all versions of Microsoft Excel

Using your mouse to select an entire list can sometimes be a little challenging, especially if (a) you have a large list because you have drag to last cell at precisely the right moment and/or (b) you're using a laptop's touch pad. Instead, use this extremely handy keyboard shortcut to select your entire list in an instant.

To quickly select a range of data

1. Click any cell within the data you want selected.
2. Use the [CTRL]+[A] keyboard shortcut.

To select your entire worksheet, do one of the following

1. After you select a range of data as seen in the previous step, use [CTRL]+[A] again. In other words, when you are in a cell with data, if you use [CTRL]+[A] twice (once to select the range and a second time to select the entire worksheet), you'll be able to select your entire worksheet.
   OR
2. Click in an empty cell anywhere in your worksheet and use the [CTRL]+[A] keyboard shortcut.
   OR
3. Click the empty header tab to the left of Column A and above Row 1, as seen below.

	A	B	C	D	E	F
1			Sales by Channel			
2						
3		Jan	Feb	Mar	Apr	May
4	Catalog	$ 35,220	$ 26,162	$ 31,809	$ 45,949	$ 22,255
5	Online	$ 51,007	$ 66,193	$ 69,480	$ 70,162	$ 64,348
6	Reseller	$ 38,512	$ 47,688	$ 50,372	$ 52,414	$ 42,583
7	Store	$ 162,066	$ 267,533	$ 229,591	$ 267,743	$ 151,837
8	Total	$ 286,806	$ 407,575	$ 381,252	$ 436,267	$ 281,023

Figure 77. Use the corner button to select the entire worksheet.

© 2019 Vickie Sokol Evans, MCT; The Red Cape Company, LLC. All Rights Reserved.

Tip #43   Use AutoFit to resize columns and rows
Applies to all versions of Microsoft Excel

There will be times when the standard column width is too narrow to display all the contents in a column. You can easily resize a column either with the mouse or by right-clicking and choosing Column Width. But what if you have multiple columns that need to be resized all at once? What if the rows need to be resized as well? You do not want to have to visit every single column and every single row to manually resize them – that would take a lot of time and eventually become very frustrating. Instead, use a feature called AutoFit.

To resize one column using AutoFit

1. Suppose you need to resize Column A. Position your cursor on the right-most edge of column A, which is the vertical line between Column A and Column B, so that your mouse turns into a double-headed arrow.
2. Next, double-click on the double-headed vertical line that separates the two columns. Excel will automatically resize the left column to the width of the cell that has the longest value or string.

To resize one row using AutoFit

- Autofit works for rows, too! When you double-click the horizontal line between two rows, Excel will apply the Best Fit to the row above the horizontal line.

To resize all columns and all rows using AutoFit

1. Select the **entire worksheet** as seen in Figure 78.

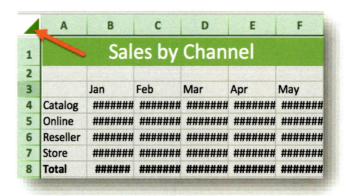

Figure 78. Entire worksheet is selected.

2. Hover over the line between two column headers, such as between A and B to get the double-headed arrow and then double-click the vertical line that separates the columns.
3. To AutoFit the rows, hover over the line between two rows to get the double-headed arrow and then double-click the horizontal line that separates the rows.

This tip meets a MOS certification exam objective.

Tip #44   Instantly add today's date and time using keyboard shortcuts
Applies to all versions of Microsoft Excel

With a few easy keyboard shortcuts, you can enter the current date and time as static values in your worksheet. Static means that the values will not update automatically.

To instantly add today's date using shortcuts

1. Click the cell where you want the current date to appear.
2. Use the [CTRL]+[;] keyboard shortcut.

To instantly add the current time using shortcuts

1. Click in the cell where you want the current time to appear.
2. Use the [CTRL]+[SHIFT]+[;] keyboard shortcut.

To instantly add the current date and time both in the same cell using shortcuts

1. Click in the cell where you want the date and time to appear.
2. Type [CTRL]+[;] then [SPACE] then [CTRL]+[SHIFT]+[;] and press [ENTER].

Manage your data with minimal effort.

First introduced in Excel 2007 for PC, Format as a Table is one of the most valuable and time saving features in Excel. With Format as a Table:

- Filter and sort features are automatically applied
- Instantly formats the entire table at once
- Includes a total row using a toggle button
- Creates calculated columns with minimal effort
- Instantly see table headers when you scroll to new pages
- Easily selects and rearranges columns
- New columns and rows are automatically added to the defined table range
- Deletes rows in your table without affecting surrounding rows in other tables
- Removes duplicates easily
- You can name your table to keep your data organized, to use as a shortcut and to use as a reference for PivotTables and Charts

As you can see, there are numerous benefits to formatting your list as a table but there are also a few limitations as well. You will need to convert your table back to a range by clicking the **Convert to Range** button on the **Table** tab in the **Tools** group if you want to do the following:

- Use the Subtotals feature
- Transpose the data

Tip #45   Format a list as a table

Introduced in Excel 2007

Before you can reap the many benefits of a table, you must first format your list as a table.

To format your list as a table

1. Click in one cell within your data.
2. On the **HOME** tab, in the **STYLES** group, click the **FORMAT AS TABLE** button to launch the table styles drop-down menu. Select the first one in the list to get started. You can always change it later.
3. Make sure the range of data you want to format as a list is correct and that it has the correct setting for **MY TABLE HAS HEADERS**. Then click **OK**.

96   © 2019 Vickie Sokol Evans, MCT; The Red Cape Company. All Rights Reserved.

Figure 79. Format As Table dialog box

Four immediate benefits of your new table

- **Filter buttons for filtering and sorting** – filter buttons are automatically added to the header row saving you time from having to insert them yourself.
- **Banded rows** – You can see the data in your table so much easier with the alternating shaded rows that used to take forever to create before Tables.
- **Table headers become column headers** – When you scroll down your table, notice how default column labels are replaced with the table headers so that (a) you can easily see the actual column name and (b) you can sort and filter from anywhere in the table without having to freeze the top row.
- **Table styles** – you can easily change the look of your table using the built-in tables styles that are connected to your Theme colors. For more information about Themes and colors see Tip #21 through o.

To find data using Autofilter

Filtering allows you to easily find and work with a subset of records in your table. It shows the records that meet your criteria and hide the records that do not. You can even filter on multiple columns.

When you format your list as a table, filter buttons are automatically added to the header row saving you time from having to insert them yourself.

1. With your data formatted as a table from the previous step, click one of the drop-down arrows next to a column in your header row.
2. Use any one or a combination of filters to find your data.

A quicker way to filter is typing the criteria for the filter in the search box rather than scrolling through a long list of values.

© 2019 Vickie Sokol Evans, MCT; The Red Cape Company, LLC. All Rights Reserved.

To change the look of your table using Table Styles

You do not have to be a graphic designer or have an eye for color to turn your table of data into a professional and eye-catching report that people will actually read. Let Excel do all the work for you using table styles, and rely on gallery previews in Excel to save even more time by showing you what the table will look like before you apply the style.

1. With your list formatted as a table, click inside your table so that the **TABLE TOOLS** contextual tab is displayed.
2. On the **DESIGN** tab in the **TABLE STYLES** group, hover over any one of the Table Styles to preview a table style.
3. Click the **MORE** button on the ribbon, as seen in Figure 80, to display more table style formats.

Figure 80. Table Styles More button

4. When you find the one you like, simply click on the style to apply.

==This tip meets a MOS certification exam objective.==

Tip #46   Expand the table as you type

Introduced in Excel 2007Once your list is formatted as a table, you can use many of the timesaving and error-reducing features of Excel tables, oe of which is AutoExpansion. As you add text to a column or to a row next to a table, Excel will automatically include that column or row in the table. In most cases, this is extremely convenient and helpful. However, you always have the ability to stop expanding.

To expand the table as you type

- Start typing content in the first column or row after your table. As soon as you press [RETURN] or [TAB] or click out of the cell, Excel adds that new column to the defined table.

To reject Table AutoExpansion

- As soon as Excel expands the table to include the new column or row, you will see the AutoCorrect Options tag pop up next to your column as seen below. Click the Options tag and select **STOP AUTOMATICALLY EXPANDING TABLES** and the new data you typed will not be included with the table.

Figure 81. Table AutoExpansion dialog box

To turn off AutoExpansion altogether

1. Click the AutoCorrect Options tag to view the AutoCorrect dialog box (as seen in the previous step).
2. Uncheck the second option **AUTOMATICALLY EXPAND TABLES** and close the window.

Changing this option will turn off Table AutoExpansion in the workbook and in any workbook you have open.

To return to the "AutoFormat As You Type" setting, on to the **FILE** tab, click **OPTIONS**. Click on the **PROOFING** category on the left and click **AUTOCORRECT OPTIONS....** Click the **AUTOFORMAT AS YOU TYPE** tab and under **APPLY AS YOU WORK**, check the box next to **INCLUDE NEW ROWS AND COLUMNS IN TABLE**.

This tip meets a MOS certification exam objective.

Tip #47   Create a calculated column with minimal effort

Introduced in Excel 2007

With your data in a table, you can create a calculation in any cell and Excel will automatically copy that calculation to every cell in that column without missing a beat. When necessary, you still have the option to stop the Calculated Column feature.

To create a calculated column in your table

1. Click in any cell of the column you wish to add the calculation.
2. Add the calculation in that cell by creating a formula or function and click [ENTER] or [TAB]. Every cell in that column should now have the calculation you just created.

To decline Column AutoCalculation this one time

- As soon as Excel adds the calculation to every cell in the column, you will see the AutoCorrect Options Tag next to your column as seen in Figure 82. Click the Options Tag and select STOP AUTOMATICALLY CREATING CALCULATED COLUMN. The new calculation you typed will only apply to the original cell and will not be added to every cell in that column.

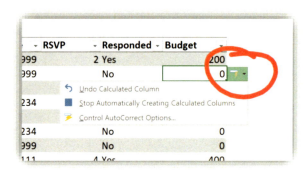

Figure 82. AutoCalculation options button.

To turn off Calculated Columns for all workbooks

1. Click the OPTIONS Tag as seen in Figure 82, and select CONTROL CALCULATED COLUMN OPTIONS…
2. In the TABLES & FILTERS dialog box as seen in Figure 83, uncheck the third option AUTOMATICALLY FILL FORMULAS and close the dialog box.

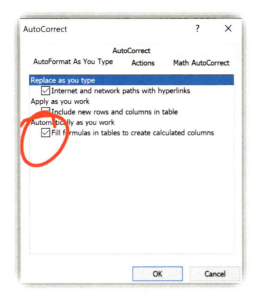

Figure 83. Turn off AutoCalculated columns for all workbooks

 Changing this option will turn off Calculated Columns in the current workbook as well as all workbooks moving forward.

 To return to the AutoFormat As You Type setting, on to the **FILE** tab, click **OPTIONS**. Click on the **PROOFING** category on the left and click **AUTOCORRECT OPTIONS…**. Click the **AUTOFORMAT AS YOU TYPE** tab and under **AUTOMATICALLY AS YOU WORK**, check the box next to **FILL FORMULAS IN TABLES TO CREATE CALCULATED COLUMNS**.

 This tip meets a MOS certification exam objective.

Tip #48   Instantly add a total row to your table

Introduced in Excel 2007

When you're ready to add a row at the bottom of your table to count the number of rows in your table or to sum a column, you can rely on your mouse clicking skills - not your math skills - to do all the work for you (Thank goodness!).

© 2019 Vickie Sokol Evans, MCT; The Red Cape Company, LLC. All Rights Reserved.

To add a total row to your table

1. With your list now formatted as a table, click anywhere in the table to activate the **TABLE TOOLS** contextual tabs.
2. On the **DESIGN** tab, in the **TABLE STYLE OPTIONS** group, click the **TOTAL ROW** option.
3. Click in any cell within your new total row and click the drop-down arrow to select the function to apply in that column.
4. To turn off the total row, click the **DESIGN** tab, and in the **TABLE STYLE OPTIONS** group and uncheck the **TOTAL ROW** option.

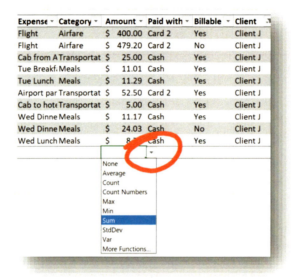

Figure 84. Within a Total Row cell, click the drop-down box to reveal popular functions.

This tip meets a MOS certification exam objective.

Tip #49 Use Slicers to quickly filter your table

Introduced in Excel 2013

Ready for something really cool? You can add Slicers to tables, which provide a fast, user-friendly, and fun way to filter your data. My students tell me that Slicers are their new favorite feature and I wholeheartedly agree! Slicers were introduced in Excel 2010, but they were only available for PivotTables to easily filter reports, with style, and control.

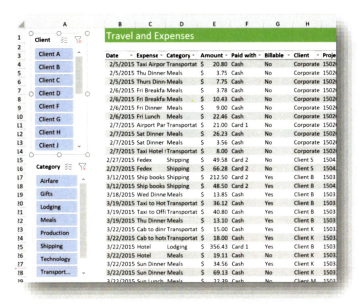

Figure 85. Two Slicers added for the Travel & Expenses Table

Tip: I like to position my slicers in either in row 1 or column A so that even if new rows or columns are added, my slicers don't get in the way. You can always resize row 1 and column A to fit your slicers, or vice versa.

To add Slicers to your table for easy filtering

1. Click anywhere in your table to activate the **TABLE TOOLS DESIGN** tab on the ribbon.
2. In the **TOOLS** group, click **INSERT SLICER** to display a list of fields available from your table.
3. Click any of the fields that you plan to use to filter your data. You can pick as many as you like. But two or three is a good start.
4. Click **OK** to view the two or three slicer boxes.
5. You can move the slicers anywhere on your worksheet and resize them.
6. Use the Slicers (one or all of them) to filter your data like magic by clicking on the values you want to filter on. Presto change-o, your table will show the filtered records!
7. To remove a filter applied to your table, click the red X on the specific slicer.

Be sure to check out the **SLICER TOOLS OPTIONS** tab in the ribbon to see how you can customize your Slicers to be different colors, multiple columns, etc. Who knew reporting in Excel could be this fun!?!

This tip meets a MOS certification exam objective.

Tip #50   Effortlessly select and move columns

Introduced in Excel 2007

Selecting just the data within a column (versus the entire column) can be tricky at times, especially if it involves scrolling to get to the end of the range. Never fear, use this one-click method to select only the data within a column and nothing more.

To select all the data in a Table column with ease

1. Suppose you want to select January sales data only. With your list now formatted as a table, position your mouse towards the top of the table column you want to select – towards the top of the word "Jan". Click as soon as your mouse turns into a down arrow as seen in Figure 86. This will select the values in the table column but not the header or total cells for that column.

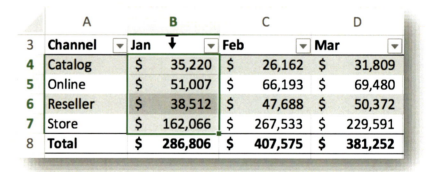

Figure 86. Select data in a table column

2. To include the header cell and the total for January, click a second time. In other words, click once for the data and twice for the data plus the column header and total cells for that table column.

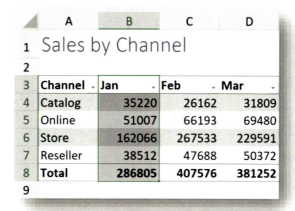

Figure 87. How to select all the data in a table column at once.

 Note: There are some cool selecting techniques unique to Tables. When you use [CTRL]+[A] within a Table, it selects the data without selecting the header and total rows. Use [CTRL]+[A] again and notice it now includes the header and total rows. [CTRL]+[A] a third time will select the entire worksheet.

The benefit of this amazing feature is that when you're copying data from one table to another, most of the time you only need the data, not the column or totals because the destination table already has the columns and the destination table will have its own dynamic total row.

To move a column with ease

1. With the table column selected (see instructions above), position your mouse on the left or right border of the selected column. Your mouse will turn into a four-headed arrow.
2. With your mouse in the shape of a four-headed arrow, click and drag the column to where you want the column to be and then let go of your mouse.

Tip #51   Remove duplicate records

Introduced in Excel 2007

 Worried about having duplicate records in your list? Thankfully, you no longer have to waste any time or risk having an inaccurate list. With your list formatted as a table, you can easily remove duplicates with just a couple of clicks!

© 2019 Vickie Sokol Evans, MCT; The Red Cape Company, LLC. All Rights Reserved.

To remove duplicate records in your table

1. With your list formatted as a table, click inside your table so that the **TABLE TOOLS** contextual tab is displayed.
2. On the **DESIGN** tab, in the **TOOLS** group, click the **REMOVE DUPLICATES** option to launch the **REMOVE DUPLICATES** dialog box seen in Figure 88.

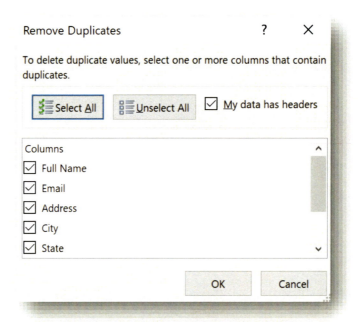

Figure 88. Remove duplicates dialog box.

3. If you want Excel to look for duplicate rows by evaluating the data in every column, use the default select all option and then click **REMOVE DUPLICATES**. Otherwise, use the checkboxes to identify which columns Excel should examine for duplicates.

This tip meets a MOS certification exam objective.

Tip #52   Summarize your data using a PivotTable

Applies to all versions of Excel

I know that they sound intimidating, but PivotTables are the most powerful yet underutilized tool in Excel. And as a matter of fact, you'll be surprised by how easy it is to create a PivotTable so that you can produce meaningful reports from one list with just a few clicks. In my opinion, every Excel user should know how to use PivotTables. In fact, according to the World Economic Forum, in collaboration with Business Insider, two of the top 10 hottest skills in 2017, are data analysis skills: #2 Statistical Analysis and Data Mining and #8 Data Presentation (Smith, 2016). Both of these skills require knowledge of PivotTables.

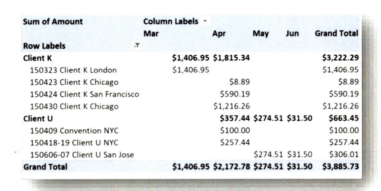

Figure 89. Example PivotTable of Monthly Billable Expense by Client Projects

To summarize your data using a PivotTable

1. Make sure your data is formatted as a table and that you select one cell within the table.
2. Click **TABLE** Tab in the Ribbon, and in the **TOOLS** group, click **SUMMARIZE WITH PIVOTTABLE** to launch the **CREATE PIVOTTABLE** dialog box as seen in Figure 90.

Figure 90. Create PivotTable dialog box

3. Confirm that the **SELECT A TABLE OR RANGE IS YOUR TABLE**, click **OK** to accept the default location. Excel will create a new worksheet in your workbook and display the PivotTable builder.
4. Click and drag data fields from the top of the builder and drop them in any of the four options at the bottom of the builder: **FILTERS, ROWS, COLUMNS** or **VALUES**. For instance, in the PivotTable report in Figure 89, I dragged the Client and Project fields to the Rows area of the Pivot. Next, Amount was added to the Values area and Date was added to the Columns area and then grouped by month.

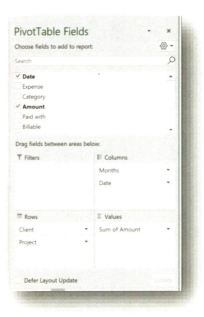

Figure 91. The PivotTable builder for Billable Client Expense report

To learn more about PivotTables, check out the on demand classes available in the RedCape Academy at www.redcapeco.com/academy/courses.

This tip meets a MOS certification exam objective.

Save time and reduce errors using magical tools.

Tip #53 Fix formatting issues using Clear Formats

Applies to all versions of Microsoft Excel

As a former Business and Data Analyst, you know what kind of data I like the most? Raw data. Nice, clean, unformatted data. It makes my life easier when creating reports because it removes any underlying issues with how the data behaves and looks.

Even if you're not an analyst, it's quite common you'll inherit someone else's data or reports that may not look or behave the way you want. In these cases, removing the formatting of your data may be the solution you need. Or maybe you may just be bored with the way your spreadsheet looks and you want to clean it up and start from scratch. Clearing the formats is a perfect, one-click remedy to eliminate unwanted formatting without compromising your data.

To clear all formatting from your data

1. Select the range of cells to remove formatting from.
2. On the **HOME** tab in the Ribbon, in the **EDITING** group, click the eraser button to view the **CLEAR** options as seen in Figure 92 below.

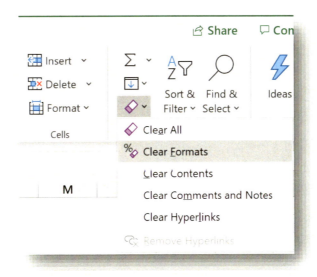

Figure 92. The Clear options available

3. Select **CLEAR FORMATS** to remove all formatting from the cells.
4. Then reformat your data as needed.

© 2019 Vickie Sokol Evans, MCT; The Red Cape Company, LLC. All Rights Reserved.   109

Tip #54 Quickly sum or count a range of cells (and show off your math skills!)

Applies to all versions of Microsoft Excel

When you need to calculate a range of cells quickly in Excel, you no longer need to invest time to create the calculation. Simply look at your status bar.

To quickly sum or count a range of cells

1. Select the range of cells in your worksheet you wish to calculate.
2. Look at your status bar at the bottom of the worksheet to view the Count, Average, and Total.

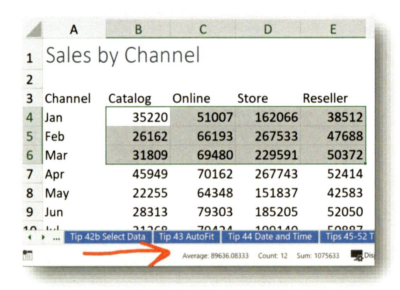

Figure 93. The Status bar displays the AutoCalculate values

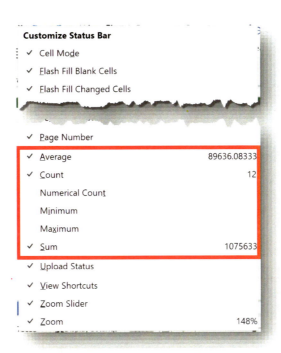

Figure 94. The Customize Status Bar window showing the AutoCalculate options

If you wish to see more calculations, right-click the status bar to display the Customize Status Bar window as seen in Figure 94 select more functions from the list of options.

Tip #55 Use Text to Columns to separate First and Last columns from a Full Name column

Applies to all versions of Microsoft Excel

When you need to separate data within a cell into multiple cells, you can use the Text to Columns feature. For example, you can separate one column with full names of customers into multiple columns that separate the first name from the last name.

Full Name
Charles McNider
Ted Kord
Wade Wilson
Roy Harper
Samuel Guthrie
Matt Murdock
Dick Greyson
Neena Thurman
Scott Lang
Jackson Day
Freida Ratsel
Arthur Douglas

Figure 95. Column of Full Names that need to be separated

To separate full names into first name and last name

1. Make sure you have several empty columns to the right of your FullName column so that Excel has a place to store the newly-separated values. You may need to insert two or three new columns.
2. Select the entire FullName column. Again, make sure there are empty columns to the right of the FullName column.
3. From the **DATA** tab, in the **DATA TOOLS** group, select **TEXT TO COLUMNS** to launch the **CONVERT TEXT TO COLUMNS WIZARD**.
4. In Step 1 of the wizard seen in Figure 96, choose **DELIMITED** and click **NEXT**.

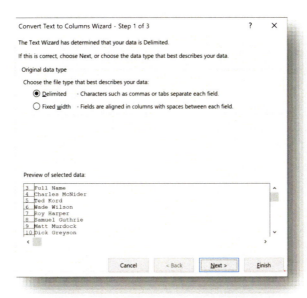

Figure 96. Convert Text to Columns Wizard - Step 1 of 3: Select Delimited

5. In Step 2 of the wizard seen in Figure 97 below, make sure **SPACE** is the only delimiter that is selected and click **NEXT**.

Figure 97. Convert to Text Columns Wizard - Step 2 of 3: Choose your delimiter, such as Space

6. In Step 3 seen in Figure 98 below, accept the default **GENERAL** setting and click **FINISH**.

© 2019 Vickie Sokol Evans, MCT; The Red Cape Company, LLC. All Rights Reserved. 113

Figure 98. Convert Text to Columns Wizard - Step 3 of 3: Confirm data type format

7. Important: before you delete any blank columns make sure they are indeed blank. Here's how…

If your data is not formatted as a Table, click on one of the names and use [CTRL]+[A] to select your new range of data. If you have any blank columns that are selected, it means that there is data somewhere in that column. Don't delete that column. You can delete any blank column after the last column in your selection as seen in Figure 99 below. In this example, Column D is the blank column that can be deleted.

If your data is formatted as a Table, use the filter buttons to confirm the values in your empty columns as seen in Figure 100.

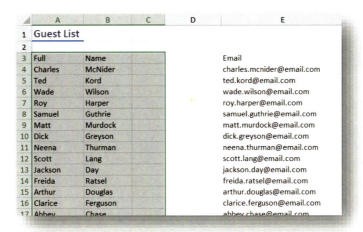

Figure 99. The range selected using [CTRL]+[A] confirms Column D is my first blank column, which can be deleted.

Figure 100. Use a column's filter button to check for data in that column.

Tip #56 Use Flash Fill to separate, combine, and create columns of data

Introduced in Excel 2013

My most favorite feature introduced in Excel 2013 is Flash Fill. I get goose bumps EVERY TIME I use it.

© 2019 Vickie Sokol Evans, MCT; The Red Cape Company, LLC. All Rights Reserved.   115

Suppose you want to create a new column in your data called Full Name. You have the first name in one column and the last name in another column. Flash fill will recognize the pattern after the first few combinations and will complete the pattern for you. Love, love, love!

Combining multiple columns has never been easier. Check it out!

To use Flash Fill to create a Full Name column

1. Assuming you have a column of first names and a column of last names (in two separate columns) create a new column called "Full Name".
2. In the first cell, start typing the full name based on the values in the First Name and Last Name column in that row.
3. In the cell right below that, type the full name for the second person based on the values in the First Name and Last Name column in that row.
4. In the cell below that, start typing the Full Name for the third person and notice that Excel begins to understand that you're taking the First and Last names and combining them.
5. Click [ENTER] to confirm the Flash Fill prediction and BAM, you're done!
6. This works for just about any other types of data clean up.
7. Try it out for the **Last, First** column. Type the last name, then a comma, then a space and then the first name for the first two people. BAM... Flash Fill should complete the rest. Goosebumps!

If Flash Fill isn't working, it may have inadvertently been turned off. In Excel, go to **Home** > **Options** > **Advanced** > under the **Editing Options** category, make sure **Automatically Flash Fill** is selected.

Tip #57 Use the Paste Special feature to perform magic and transform your data

Applies to all versions of Microsoft Excel

You can copy and paste formulas throughout your spreadsheet, but what if you want Excel to copy and paste a formula's resulting value rather than the formula itself? Use a command called "Paste Values."

You can also use Paste Values when you're pasting data from the Internet to avoid bringing in hyperlinks and internet formatting.

Keyboard Shortcut. [ALT]+[CTRL]+[V]

To paste values instead of formulas

1. Select the cells that contain the values you want.
2. On the **HOME** tab, in the **CLIPBOARD** group, click **COPY**.
3. Select the destination cell.
4. On the **HOME** tab, in the **CLIPBOARD** group, click the **PASTE DROP-DOWN ARROW** to view the drop-down menu as seen below.
5. Under the **PASTE VALUES** heading, click **PASTE VALUES**.

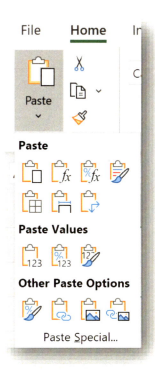

Figure 101. The Paste drop-down menu

To flip your data using transpose text

When you need to see your columns as rows and your rows as columns, you can easily flip the data using transpose text.

1. Select the data you want to flip or transpose.
2. On the **HOME** tab, in the **CLIPBOARD** group, click **COPY**.
3. Select on cell in an empty area of a worksheet, perhaps below the original data set.
4. On the **HOME** tab, in the **CLIPBOARD** group, click the Paste drop-down arrow to view the drop-down menu as seen below.
5. Under the **PASTE** heading, click the last icon called **TRANSPOSE**.

Those are just two examples of helpful Paste Special tools you can use. There are over a dozen more that will magically transform your data. I invite you to play around and test the Paste Special options by clicking **PASTE SPECIAL...** from the Paste drop-down menu.

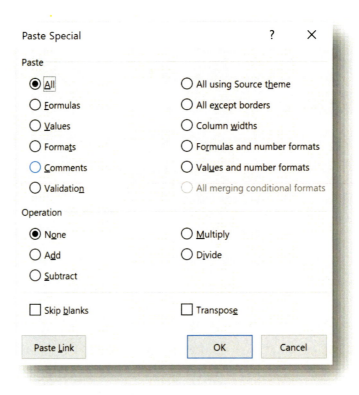

Figure 102. Paste Special dialog box

The different options available in "Paste Special" all serve unique functions:

- All – pastes the cell contents and formatting. This is the default setting.
- Formulas – pastes the formulas.
- Values – pastes the resulting values.
- Formats – pastes only the format.
- Comments – pastes the comments.
- Validation – pastes the validation drop-down list.
- All using Source theme – pastes the original theme formatting into the destination cells.
- All except borders – brings over everything but not the borders.
- Column widths – only pastes the column widths.
- Formula and number formats – pastes only the formula and the number formats but not any cell formatting such as colors and borders.

- Values and number formats – pastes the values only, plus the number formats but not colors or borders.
- All, merge conditional formats – pastes the information and keeps the conditional formatting in the destination cells.
- Add – Add the valued copied to all the selected cells and displays the new values.
- Subtract – Subtract the valued copied to all the selected cells and displays the new values.
- Multiply – Multiple the valued copied to all the selected cells and displays the new values.
- Divide – Divide the valued copied to all the selected cells and displays the new values.
- Skip Blanks – if there are blank cells in the values copied, it won't paste or overwrite cells in the resulting cells.
- Transpose – flips the data so that your column data is now in the rows and your row data is now in columns.
- Paste Link – Links the pasted data.

This tip meets a MOS certification exam objective.

Reveal critical information about your data.

Tip #58   Flag duplicate values in your column

Introduced in Excel 2007

When you need to monitor your data for duplicates, Excel's conditional formatting will do the trick. When Excel sees a duplicate value in a column, it will highlight it for you. You can even sort and filter based on those duplicate values. What fun!

To flag duplicate values

1. Select the column you wish check for duplicates.
2. On the **HOME** tab, in the **STYLES** group, click **CONDITIONAL FORMATTING**, which displays the **CONDITIONAL FORMATTING** drop-down menu.
3. Select **HIGHLIGHT CELL RULES** and then choose **DUPLICATE VALUES...**, which displays the **DUPLICATE VALUES** dialog box seen in Figure 103.

Figure 103. New Formatting Rule dialog box for finding duplicate values in a range of cells

4. Accept the default setting and click **OK**. Or you can choose a different formatting setting using the various options in the **VALUES WITH** drop-down.
5. If there are any duplicates in your column, they will be highlighted in pink (or another color if you opted not to go with the default in the previous step). See the following two procedures to quickly sort or filter your duplicate values based on the conditional formatting.

To sort the duplicates to display first

If you want your duplicate values at the top of your list, you can easily sort based on the formatting of the duplicate cells.

1. If your filter buttons aren't already turned on, turn them on now. Click anywhere in your list and from the **HOME** tab, in the **EDITING** group, click the **SORT & FILTER** button, and select **FILTER**. Filter buttons will appear in the header for each column.

Keyboard shortcut: [CTRL]+[SHIFT]+[L].

2. Click the Filter button for the column with the duplicate values you want to be at the top of the list. In my example, the **Email** column has duplicates I want to bring to the top of the list.
3. In the **SORT AND FILTER** options under Sort, click **SORT BY COLOR**. In my example, since I chose the default pink conditional format in the previous procedure, my **CELL COLOR** is pink.

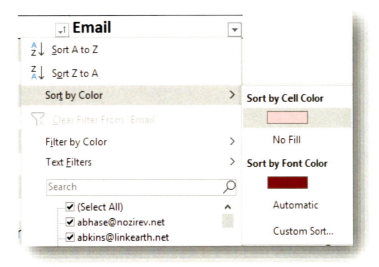

Figure 104. Sort by Cell Color using the Sort & Filter options available on the Email column.

4. Click **OK** to close the **SORT & FILTER** options window to view your duplicates at the top of your list.

Figure 105. Excel sorted the duplicates to the top of the list while keeping the other contacts sorted by last name.

5. To remove the sort, simply re-sort the column or sort on a different column.

To filter and show the rows that have duplicate values in a column

Use this procedure when you want to display only the duplicates.

1. If your filter buttons aren't already turned, turn them on. Click anywhere in your list and from the **HOME** tab, in the **EDITING** group, click the **SORT & FILTER** button and select **FILTER**.
2. Click the **FILTER** button for the column with the duplicate values you want to be at the top of the list. In my example, the **Email** column has duplicates I want to bring to the top of the list.
3. In the **SORT AND FILTER** options, under **FILTER BY COLOR**, click the arrow and choose **CELL COLOR** and then select the duplicate color. In my example, since I chose the default pink conditional format in the previous procedure, my **CELL COLOR** is pink.

Figure 106. Filter by Cell Color using Sort & Filter options available on the Email column.

4. Your list will now be filtered to show only the duplicates.

Figure 107. Filtered list to only show the rows with duplicate values in a column

5. To remove the filter, click the Filter button again for that column and select **Clear Filter from**.

This tip meets a MOS certification exam objective.

Tip #59 Use conditional formatting for Status Flags

Introduced in Excel 2007

If you're using Excel to track the progress of your projects you will inevitably need Red, Yellow, and Green status flags. These features provide an at-a-glance view of your progress. Use Excel's conditional formatting to turn the cells into dynamic flags based on the value in the cell as seen in Figure 108. When a status changes from Yellow to Green, for example, the color of the cell will change automatically to green.

Figure 108. Example Status Flags with conditional formatting

To use conditional formatting to add red, yellow and green status flags

1. Select the Status column where you are tracking the status of each task.
2. On the **HOME** tab, in the **STYLES** group, click **CONDITIONAL FORMATTING**, which displays the **CONDITIONAL FORMATTING** drop-down menu.
3. Select **HIGHLIGHT CELL RULES** and then choose **TEXT THAT CONTAINS…**, which displays the **NEW FORMATTING RULE** dialog box.
4. In the **FORMAT CELLS THAT CONTAIN THE TEXT:** blank cell type **Green** or whatever value you want Excel to search for.

Figure 109. New Formatting Rule dialog box for conditional formatting based on cells that contain specific text

5. In the **Format with** setting, click the drop-down and select **custom format…** to launch the **Format Cells** dialog box.

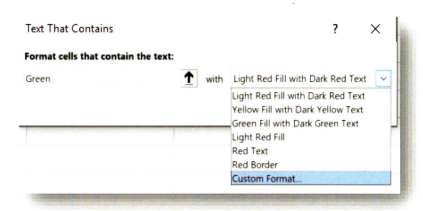

Figure 110. Choose **custom format…** from the **Format with…** drop-down.

6. Click the **Fill** tab and from the **Background color** drop-down, which is currently set to no color.
7. Under **Standard Colors**, click the Green color. Note: It is important that you select one of the green colors in the very bottom row. These are Standard Colors because they are static and don't change.

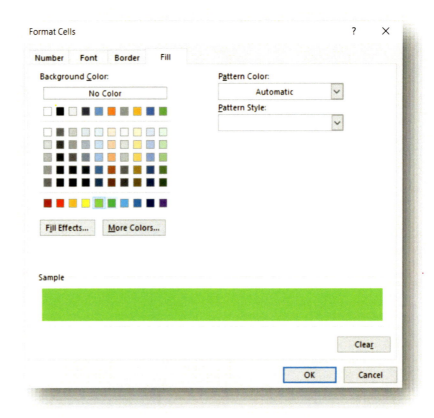

Figure 111 Change the Background color to a Standard Color green.

 Important! Do not select a green above the last row. Those colors are Theme Colors, which are dynamic and will change if you or your colleague changes the global Theme colors of the workbook. You should ALWAYS use the Standard Colors (the last row) for status tags because they are static colors, which aren't connected to Themes. For more information about Theme Colors, see Tips 15-16.

8. Next, click the **Font** tab at the top of the **Format Cells** dialog box and make sure the **Color** is white or black based on what you need.
9. Click **OK**.
10. Repeat these steps for each status flag color you have.

 This tip meets a MOS certification exam objective.

Tip #60   Use a heat map to track your progress

Introduced in Excel 2007

One of the many ways you can immediately see the story behind your data is to use conditional formatting, specifically a heat map. Heat maps are a visual summary of your data that communicate the relationship between values that you wouldn't be able to immediately see with data alone.

For instance, compare the two reports in Figure 112 below. One is obviously using a heat map. Which one of the reports answers the following two questions quickly and effectively: (1) Which survey categories have the highest ratings? (2) Which ones have the lowest ratings? Notice how we can easily track our progress and identify issues with the business with a heat map.

Survey Report		Survey Report w/ Heat Map	
Survey Category	**Rating**	**Survey Category**	**Rating**
Attendees	18	Attendees	18
Overall	6.34	Overall	6.34
Instructor	6.86	Instructor	6.86
Courseware	6.78	Courseware	6.78
Environment	6.33	Environment	6.33
Learning Effectiveness	6.89	Learning Effectiveness	6.89
Job Impact	6.88	Job Impact	6.88
Alignment	6.29	Alignment	6.29
Business Results	6.47	Business Results	6.47
Support Tools	5.43	Support Tools	5.43
Return on Investment	6.71	Return on Investment	6.71

Figure 112. Example heat map compared to a report without a heat map

To create a heat map of your values

1. Select the all the values you wish to evaluate.
2. On the **HOME** tab, in the **STYLES** group, click the **CONDITIONAL FORMATTING** drop-down.

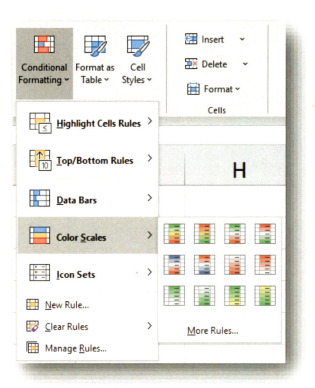

Figure 113. Heat Map options using Color Scales conditional formatting

3. In the **COLOR SCALES** category, click the first one to apply the basic heat map colors to your data where the highest number will be green and the lowest red.
4. Select the one you prefer. The colors will represent a variance so that you can easily spot values that are outside the average range of numbers.

To remove the heat map, select the range again. On the **HOME** tab, in the **STYLES** group, click the **CONDITIONAL FORMATTING** drop-down, highlight **CLEAR RULES** and then select **CLEAR RULES FROM SELECTED CELLS**.

This tip meets a MOS certification exam objective.

Tip #61   Effortlessly create a chart

Applies to all versions of Microsoft Excel

When working in Excel, there are many times when the hardest part is just getting started. The easiest way to get started with a chart is by using a keyboard shortcut or choosing from a list of recommended charts.

To create a chart at the press of a button

1. Select the range you want to chart.
2. Press [F11] on your keyboard to launch a basic bar chart on a new worksheet.
3. Use the **CHART TOOLS** contextual tab on the Ribbon to modify your new chart.

To create a chart using recommended charts from the Ribbon

The [F11] shortcut above only gives you one chart option, which can be a great start. But if you want a selection of recommended charts, Excel gives you some really smart options that would have taken you significant time to even dream up, if you ever even thought of them at all.

1. With your data selected, on the **INSERT** tab in the **CHARTS** group, click **RECOMMENDED CHARTS**, which launches the **INSERT CHART** dialog box seen in Figure 114.

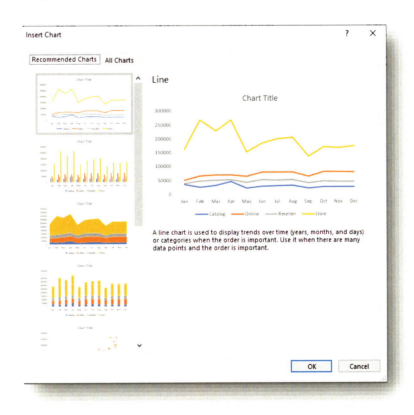

Figure 114. Recommended charts for the sales data selected

2. Scroll through all of the charts on the left to find the one that tells the most compelling story about your data. You can click each chart to see a preview of the chart. To see more charts, select the "All Charts" tab.
3. Once you find the one you want, click **OK** and Excel will insert the chart in your current spreadsheet.
4. Use the Chart ribbons to make changes to your new chart.

To create a chart using recommend charts Quick Analysis Tool

Introduced in Excel 2013, the Quick Analysis tool appears in the right-hand corner of the selected data as seen in Figure 115. Clicking this button allows you to create the chart you want in just a few clicks as well as other cool things.

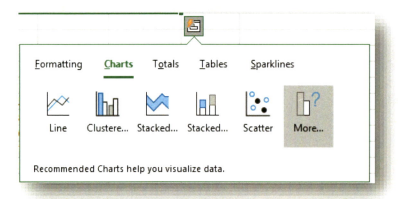

Figure 115. The Quick Analysis Tool

  Keyboard Shortcut. [CONTROL]+[Q]

1. Select the range of data you want to analyze using a chart.
2. The Quick Analysis Tool icon will appear at the bottom right-hand corner of the selected text. If not, use the shortcut key [CONTROL]+[Q].
3. Click the **CHARTS** tab and hover over each one of the chart types to see a preview of your data as that chart type, as seen in Figure 116.

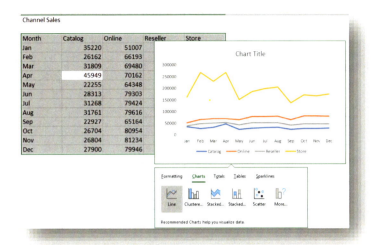

Figure 116. A preview of the line chart using the Quick Analysis Tool

4. Click the chart you want and Excel will place the new chart in your worksheet.
5. With each chart, you'll get contextual ribbon tabs with various commands. Use the Chart ribbons to make changes to your new chart.

This tip meets a MOS certification exam objective.

Tip #62 See the trend in each row using Sparklines

Introduced in Excel 2010

Sparklines are tiny charts that reside in a cell to show trends and the story behind your data quickly and easily. For example, looking at this report, which channels, if any, trended upward last year? Overall, did the year trend upwards or downwards?

Channel Sales	Q1	Q2	Q3	Q4	Total
Catalog	$ 93,191	$ 96,517	$ 85,956	$ 81,408	$ 357,072
Online	$ 186,680	$ 213,813	$ 224,204	$ 242,135	$ 866,831
Reseller	$ 136,573	$ 147,046	$ 144,201	$ 139,793	$ 567,612
Store	$ 659,190	$ 604,784	$ 542,170	$ 513,970	$ 2,320,115

Figure 117. Report without Sparklines

Now look at the same report but with Sparklines added. Which channels, if any, trended upward last year? Overall, did the year trend upwards or downwards?

	Q1	Q2	Q3	Q4	Total	Trendline
Channel Sales						
Catalog	$ 93,191	$ 96,517	$ 85,956	$ 81,408	$ 357,072	
Online	$ 186,680	$ 213,813	$ 224,204	$ 242,135	$ 866,831	
Reseller	$ 136,573	$ 147,046	$ 144,201	$ 139,793	$ 567,612	
Store	$ 659,190	$ 604,784	$ 542,170	$ 513,970	$ 2,320,115	

Figure 118. Report with Sparklines

The answers are clear: Online Sales was the only channel that trended upward, and there was a downward trend in sales overall.

Here's another example of a Sparkline. As you can see below, Washington outdid the other two states during the entire year except in July when California had the highest sales. Including the Sparklines in these reports makes it so much easier to see what happened over the year and help make better business decisions.

	New York	Dallas	Chicago	
Jan	$ 8,339	$ 7,548	$ 15,846	
Feb	$ 7,545	$ 7,825	$ 14,053	
Mar	$ 8,580	$ 8,159	$ 14,977	
Apr	$ 9,428	$ 9,119	$ 14,408	
May	$ 9,972	$ 8,426	$ 13,133	
Jun	$ 11,332	$ 9,526	$ 12,911	
Jul	$ 12,184	$ 10,050	$ 11,394	
Aug	$ 11,962	$ 9,370	$ 12,088	
Sep	$ 11,447	$ 9,902	$ 11,733	
Oct	$ 10,023	$ 9,954	$ 12,154	
Nov	$ 13,837	$ 9,790	$ 14,337	
Dec	$ 14,219	$ 14,964	$ 19,940	

Figure 119. Example report with Column Sparklines

To create a Sparkline chart

1. Select the first empty cell to the right of your range of data.
2. On the **INSERT** tab, in the **SPARKLINES** group, click **LINE**, **BAR** or **WIN/LOSS**.

3. Click in the **DATA RANGE** text field and with your mouse, highlight the range for which you want to view the trend. Hint: be sure not to include the final year-end total if you have one. For instance, in Figure 120, I only selected Q1 through Q4 Catalog sales. I did not include the Total for Catalog Sales.

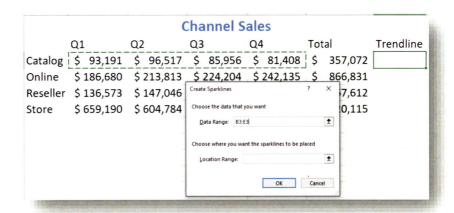

Figure 120. Create Sparklines dialog box

4. Click **OK**.
5. Using the Autofill handle of the cell with the new Sparkline chart, copy the Sparkline down the other cells if necessary. See Tip #41 for help with Autofill.
6. Use the **SPARKLINE DESIGN** ribbon to customize the look and behavior of your Sparkline chart.

This tip meets a MOS certification exam objective.

Share nicely with others.

Tip #63   Prevent columns from printing across two pages
Applies to all versions of Microsoft Excel

You've been there. Ready to print your amazing spreadsheet only to see the columns break across two pages. And no matter how hard you try – and you try really, really hard – it's almost impossible to get the font small enough so that all of your columns make it onto the first page and large enough to actually read it.

Reports can carry over rows and rows of data to another page vertically. But split the columns across multiple tables? Only in rare instances.

Put away your magnifying glass and the tape! There's a simple trick. Let's set the width for your report to one page and leave the height to Automatic.

Also, whether you are doing your part to save the environment or you're out of printer ink and staples, you can print your entire spreadsheet on one page with minimal effort as well.

To print all columns on one page

1. On the **PAGE LAYOUT** tab, in the **SCALE TO FIT** group, change the **WIDTH** drop-down to 1 page as seen in Figure 121.

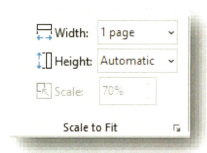

Figure 121. Page Width settings on the Page Layout tab

2. Use Print Preview to check your work or use [CTRL]+[P].
3. If the data is now too small, change the margins to **NARROW MARGINS** and perhaps change the settings for the page orientation and page size until you get the exact look you want, as seen in Figure 122.

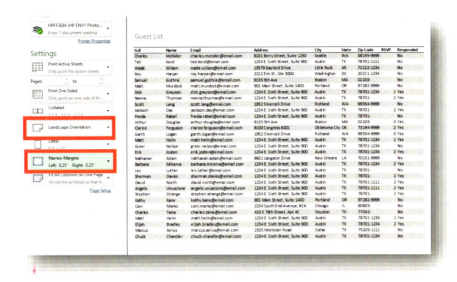

Figure 122. Print preview settings for page orientation and margins

To print your entire report on one page

- On the **Page Layout** tab, in the **Page Setup** group, change both the **Width** drop-down and the **Height** drop-down to **1 page**.

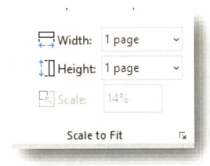

Figure 123. Page and Height Width set to print on one page

- Or go to the **File** tab and click **Print** and then change the **Scaling** setting to **Fit Sheet on One Page** as seen in Figure 124.

Figure 124. Fit Sheet on One Page scaling option in the Print window

This tip meets a MOS certification exam objective.

Tip #64   Print column headings to show on each page

Applies to all versions of Microsoft Excel

Now that you've learned to how keep all your columns on one page instead of splitting across multiple pages, it's time to focus on the rows. It's acceptable for the rows to split across multiple pages, vertically. But when it happens we need to make sure that when you have column headings, they are repeated on every page. Here's how.

Print column headings on every page

1. On the **PAGE LAYOUT** tab, in the **PAGE SETUP** group, click **PRINT TITLES** as seen in Figure 125.

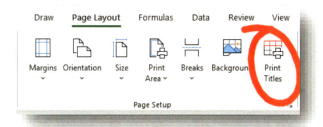

Figure 125. Print Titles command on the Page Layout ribbon

2. Click in the **ROWS TO REPEAT AT TOP** field. Then, click on row letter for the row you want to repeat on every page. For instance, in Figure 126, I need row 1 to repeat on every page. Once selected, Excel will place the appropriate reference to that row (or rows) in the **PRINT TITLES** setting.

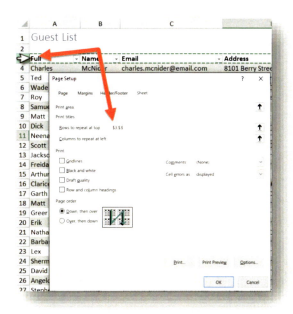

Figure 126. Print Titles setting in the Page Setup dialog box

3. Click **OK**.

Tip #65   Send a worksheet - not the entire workbook - to a colleague
Applies to all versions of Microsoft Excel

When you need to send a colleague your spreadsheet, but you don't want to send the entire workbook, copy the one worksheet they need to a new workbook and then send the new workbook (with that one worksheet) to your colleague.

To copy a worksheet to a new workbook

1. Right-click the sheet tab you wish to share and choose **MOVE OR COPY…**
2. Click the **TO BOOK:** drop-down and select **(NEW BOOK)**.
3. Very important! Check the box **CREATE A COPY** as seen in Figure 127.

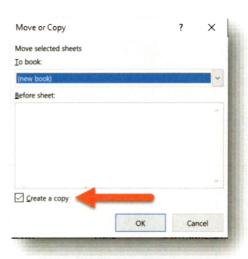

Figure 127. Move or copy worksheet dialog box: This option MUST be checked

4. Click **OK**. The title bar at the top of your worksheet should say Book1 or similar, herein referred to as Book#.
5. Go back to your original workbook and confirm that the sheet was copied (as described in Step 3) and that the sheet is still in the original workbook.

To send the worksheet as an email attachment

1. Make sure you are in the new Book# workbook.
2. On the **FILE** tab, click **SHARE** (or **SEND**, depending on your version).
3. Click **EMAIL**, then click **SEND AS ATTACHMENT** or **SEND AS PDF** and complete your email message.
4. Return to Book# and save, if necessary, or close without saving only after you have confirmed the sheet you just emailed is still in your original workbook.

This tip meets a MOS certification exam objective.

Chapter References

Smith, J. (2016, October 25). *Mastering these skills could get you hired in 2017*. Retrieved from www.weforum.org: https://www.weforum.org/agenda/2016/10/2017s-most-in-demand-skills-according-to-linkedin

Chapter 5:
Microsoft PowerPoint Tips

Save time, eliminate unessential work (and bad habits), ensure consistency throughout your presentations, use your corporate brand with confidence, reduce mistakes, effectively communicate your message, improve your design skills, and meet your deadline.

In this Chapter

- Organize your presentation to make it easier to build and craft a compelling message
- Discover essential shortcuts and hacks to transform your presentation and meet critical deadlines
- Save time and eliminate embarrassing errors by repurposing content, slides, designs, themes and templates

Don't reinvent the wheel.

Tip #66   Use a Theme to define your colors, fonts, and layouts

Applies to all versions of Microsoft PowerPoint

Hands-down, Themes is the number-one timesaving feature in PowerPoint. *Every* PowerPoint user should understand what Themes are and how to use them properly. And *every* marketing department should create, program, and deploy a Theme for their employees to use directly from the ribbon.

So what exactly is a Theme? Essentially, it's the design or brand used for your slides. It's what the presentation should "look" like.

Themes include slide layouts (including logos and graphics), backgrounds, colors, fonts and effects. The Theme determines where your company logo shows up as you progress through your slides, footer information, graphics, where text and images are positioned on the slides, what colors flow through the presentation, and the one to two fonts that you can use. Using Themes ensures consistency, saves development time, and helps you adhere to your company's brand. Themes are stored in the Ribbon instead of on the company intranet. One-click and you've got everything you need.

© 2019 Vickie Sokol Evans, MCT The Red Cape Company, LLC. All Rights Reserved.   141

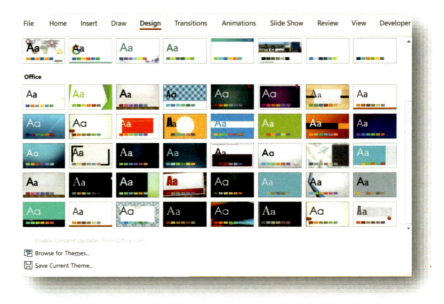

Figure 128. Themes gallery showing my custom Themes

For example, in the screenshot above in the top row, I've personally created 8 custom Themes for training purposes. These are training examples I built just for fun for brands such as: Contoso (a fictitious company), FedEx, Facebook, Google, and Microsoft. They aren't the real corporate Themes for these companies. They were created just for training purposes.

If you're not into building Themes from scratch, PowerPoint comes with over 40 Themes you can use for your presentation and 4 Variations for each Theme. That means you have over 160 designs to choose from!

To use a design theme that comes with PowerPoint

Until your corporate Theme is available in the PowerPoint Ribbon like the examples above, you can start with one of the many Themes that come with PowerPoint.

1. Start PowerPoint and click **BLANK PRESENTATION**. Or, if you are already in PowerPoint, use [CTRL]+[N] to launch a new presentation.
2. On the **DESIGN** tab in the **THEMES** group, hover over the various Themes available.
3. When you find a Theme you like, click the theme to apply to all slides. In this example, I chose the "Banded" theme as seen in Figure 129.

Figure 129. Selecting the "Banded" Theme for my presentation

Use a variation of the Theme

Each Theme that comes with PowerPoint has four variations. These variations were introduced in PowerPoint 2013 and provide color and background options for the current Theme seen in Figure 130. Most Themes (but not all) will include the following variants:

- One color background
- A white background
- A dark background
- A fourth option

Variants don't affect the font or design, just the color palette being used and the subsequent backgrounds.

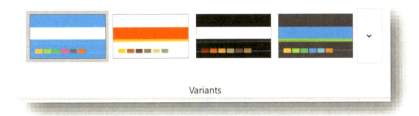

Figure 130. Variants available for the "Banded" Theme

1. After you select your Theme, try out one of the four variations that come with each theme: On the **DESIGN** tab, in the **VARIANTS** group, hover over one of the variants to get an idea of what is available.

2. Then click the variant you want to apply. In this example, I chose the variant with the white background as seen in Figure 131.

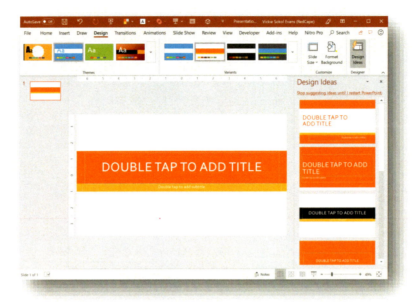

Figure 131. The Variant I chose for the "Banded" Theme

Select your colors

1. If you're happy with the colors in the Theme variation, then skip this step. Otherwise, on the **Design** tab in the **Variants** group, click the drop-down for the Variants and select **Colors** to view the Color Sets available as seen in Figure 132.

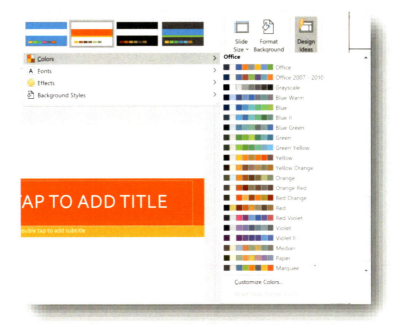

Figure 132. Color sets available in PowerPoint

2. Hover over the color sets to preview the colors in your presentation.
3. Click one of the color sets to apply to the presentation. I chose the **Red Violet** Color Set seen in Figure 133.

Figure 133. The Red Violet color set applied to the "Banded" Theme

To create your own Color Set, click **CUSTOMIZE COLORS** at the bottom of your Colors list and use your company's RGB color settings to set up your color palette. Name the new color set using your Company Name. Your new Color Set will now be available across all Office applications.

For more information about creating custom Color Sets and Themes, attend the *Office Themes* and *Slide Masters* courses available in The RedCape Academy: www.redcapeco.com/academy.

In Excel 2010 or earlier, on the **DESIGN** tab, in the **THEMES** group, click the **COLORS** drop-down option to view all the Color Sets.

Select your fonts

1. Now it's time to select the one (or two) fonts you will use throughout your presentation. On the **DESIGN** tab, in the **VARIANTS** group, click the drop-down for the Variants and select **FONTS**.

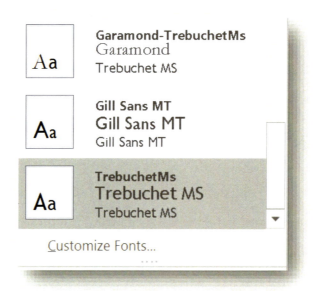

Figure 134. Font Sets available in PowerPoint

2. Hover over the font sets to preview the fonts.
3. Click one of the font sets to apply. I chose **Trebuchet MS** for my example.

In Excel 2010 or earlier, on the **Design** tab, in the **Themes** group, click the **Fonts** drop-down option to view all the Font Sets.

This tip meets a MOS certification exam objective.

Tip #67 Reuse and merge slides from other presentations

Applies to all versions of Microsoft PowerPoint

When you want to add slides from another presentation into your current presentation, you can simply Copy and Paste between presentations. But you must decide on the format for those new slides. Do you want the slides to keep their original formatting (from the source presentation) or do you want them to look like the slides in the current presentation (the destination presentation)? In most cases you want the latter. You want the slides you're pasting to take on the design of your current presentation.

The default behavior for copying and pasting is for PowerPoint to use the destination Theme/format. It will not bring in the source file's design Theme. But it will bring over any direct formatting on the slide(s).

If you want the slides to keep their original format/brand, then you'll want to keep the source formatting.

Format	Method
Use the destination format/Theme	Use default **Copy/Paste**
Keep the source file's format/Theme	Use **Copy/Paste Special** (keep source formatting)

To copy/paste slides from another presentation and use **destination** formatting

1. In the source file, select and copy the slides you want to bring into your destination file.
2. Since you want the slides you're copying to take on the format of the destination file, simply paste them into the destination file.

© 2019 Vickie Sokol Evans, MCT The Red Cape Company, LLC. All Rights Reserved.

To copy/paste slides from another presentation and keep source formatting

1. In the source file, select and copy the slides you want to bring into your destination file.
2. In the destination file, navigate where you want the new slide(s) to be. On the **Home** tab, click the **Paste** drop-down arrow and choose **Keep Source Formatting**.

This tip meets a MOS certification exam objective.

Manage your presentation.

Tip #68   Create sections in PowerPoint

Introduced in PowerPoint 2010

Sections allow you to group slides together so that you can nicely organize your topics or speaker slides, effortlessly navigate your presentation, and easily print logical sections of slides. It was one of MY favorite features introduced in PowerPoint 2010.

Here is an example of a 27-slide presentation with sections defined for each speaker.

- Introduction (3 slides)
- Mr. London (7 slides)
- Mr. Sydney (5 slides)
- Ms. Austin (6 slides)
- Partner Spotlight (4 slides)
- Q&A + Wrap Up (2 slides)

You can also create sections centered on topics or the schedule for the day (i.e. Session 1, Break, Session 2…). Section your slides in a way that will help you organize the slides behind the scenes as well as navigate while presenting.

To create sections in your presentation

1. In either Normal or Slide Sorter view, click on the first slide you want in the new section or click in the space in between slides where you want your section.
2. On the **HOME** tab, in the **SLIDES** group, click **SECTION**.
3. Select **ADD SECTION** to create a new section after the current slide. Alternatively, you can right-click in front of a slide and choose **ADD SECTION**.
4. Give your section a meaningful name such as the topic or speaker name.
5. Repeat the steps above to create more sections throughout your presentation.

Tip: Right-click any section name to see all the commands you have available for sections as seen in Figure 135. You can rename sections, expand and collapse sections, move sections of slides around, as well as delete a section or delete a section along with its slides.

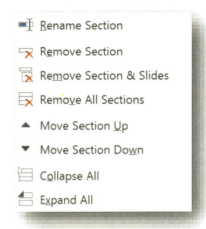

Figure 135. Section commands available when you right-click a section

To print one section of slides

1. Go to the **FILE** tab, click **PRINT** and click the **PRINT ALL SLIDES** drop-down to reveal the list of options. You will see a heading called Sections and all of your sections will be listed there as seen in Figure 136.
2. Click the Section you want to print and then configure the rest of the printing such as full slides or handouts, etc.

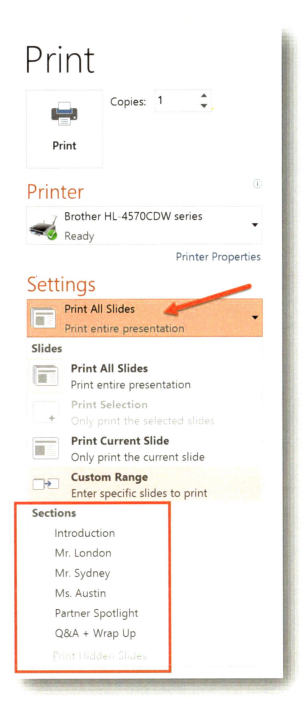

Figure 136. Print Dialog Box to print sections

This tip meets a MOS certification exam objective.

Tip #69 Use the new Zoom feature to create summary slides and navigation

Introduced in PowerPoint 2016

Hands down, this is my favorite new feature of PowerPoint 2016! Although, it's only for those with an Office 365 subscription.

The Zoom feature allows you to instantly create a dynamic summary slide at the beginning of your presentation based on slides that already exist, as seen here in Figure 137.

Figure 137. Summary slide example using the new Zoom feature

Benefits of the Summary Zoom include:

- It serves as your table of contents.
- Each item on the slide is a hyperlink to that section of the presentation.
- It gives you the ability to navigate and present your sections in any order.
- After you go through a section, PowerPoint takes you back to the main summary slide. You can turn this off if you'd like.
- The summary slide is dynamic, so when you change content on the original slide, the slide on the summary will automatically update

To create a Summary Zoom slide

This is much easier if you have sections in your presentation. If you don't have sections in your presentation, return to Tip #68 to add your sections and then complete these steps:

1. From anywhere within your PowerPoint presentation, on the **INSERT** tab in the **LINKS** group click the **ZOOM** drop-down and select **SUMMARY ZOOM** as seen in Figure 138.

Figure 138. Insert Summary Zoom command on the Insert Ribbon

2. In the **INSERT SUMMARY ZOOM** dialog box, the first slide in each one of my sections is selected automatically as seen in Figure 139. If you didn't have sections, nothing would be selected and you would have the ability to select each of the slides to include in the Summary Zoom.

Figure 139. Insert Summary Zoom dialog box with Section Header Slides selected

3. When you are done selecting the slides you want in the Summary Zoom, click **INSERT**. A new section called **Summary Section** is created at the beginning of your presentation along with the Summary Zoom slide as seen in Figure 140.

Figure 140. New Summary Section and Summary Zoom slide

A close-up of the Summary Zoom slide shows the six Section Header slides included in the Summary, as seen in Figure 141.

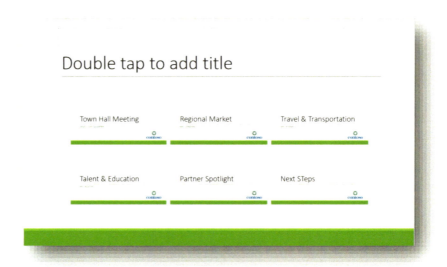

Figure 141. The new Summary Zoom slide

4. Click in the Slide Title placeholder and add a title to your slide such as **Summary** or **Where do you want to go?**

5. To see what the Summary Zoom slide does, run your presentation from the beginning and click on any one of the items on the slide to navigate through the presentation. Notice that after you finish a section, PowerPoint takes you back to the Summary Zoom slide.

To format your Summary Zoom slide

1. On your Summary Zoom slide, click the Zoom placeholder to activate the Zoom Tools. On the **ZOOM TOOLS FORMAT** tab in the **ZOOM STYLES** group, select any one of the Zoom Styles to give your Summary Zoom a new look. I chose **ROTATED WHITE** as seen in Figure 142.

Figure 142. Zoom Styles

The final version of my Summary Zoom can be seen in Figure 143.

Figure 143. The final version of my Summary Zoom

2. If you don't want PowerPoint to return to your Summary Zoom slide after each section, you can turn that off. On the **ZOOM TOOLS FORMAT** tab, in the **ZOOM OPTIONS** group, uncheck **RETURN TO ZOOM** as seen in Figure 144.

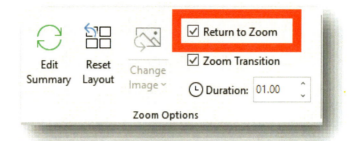

Figure 144. Return to Zoom check box on the Zoom Tools Format tab

3. To edit which slides show up in the Summary Zoom, on the **Zoom Tools Format** tab, **Zoom Options** group, click **Edit Summary** as seen in Figure 145.

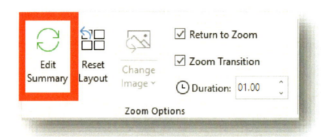

Figure 145. Edit Summary command on the Zoom Tools Format tab

Tip #70 Create one slide show for multiple audiences
Applies to all versions of Microsoft PowerPoint

Rather than creating multiple files of your presentation for different audiences or hiding slides within your presentation, you can create one PowerPoint file that includes multiple slide shows for various audiences.

For example, an executive audience might only need to see the high-level overview slides and then another audience needs to see both the high-level overview and the more detailed slides. You can do this without hiding slides and without having to create and manage two separate slide decks.

To create a custom slide show for each audience

1. On the **Slide Show** tab, in the **Start Slide Show** group, click **Custom Slide Show**.
2. Click **New…**
3. In the Define New Slide Show window, as seen in Figure 146, type a name that best describes the custom slide show in the **Slide Show Name** box.

4. From the **SLIDES IN PRESENTATION** list, select the slide you want to include in the custom slide show and click the **ADD** button. Repeat for all the slides you need for this custom slide show.
5. Use the move up and move down buttons to reorder the slides in the list.
6. When done, click **OK** and **CLOSE**.
7. Repeat for each custom presentation.

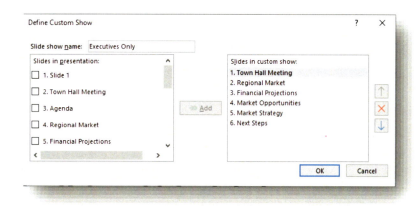

Figure 146. Define Custom Slide Show dialog box

To launch a custom slide show

1. On the **SLIDE SHOW** tab, in the **START SLIDE SHOW** group, click **CUSTOM SLIDE SHOW**.
2. Select the custom show you wish to run.
3. Click **SHOW**.

    Or

1. Use the [F5] keyboard shortcut to run your main slide show.
2. Right-click the current slide and hover over **CUSTOM SHOW**.
3. Select the custom show you wish to run.

This tip meets a MOS certification exam objective.

Work smarter and reduce panic attacks.

Tip #71 Save hours by using layouts

Applies to all versions of Microsoft PowerPoint

Many of the world's problems would be solved if presenters used the correct layout for their slides. Of course, I'm exaggerating - but it certainly will save hours of time and frustration, result in a more professional presentation, help you meet deadlines, and get you home on time.

Slide layouts provide instant structure to your slides because they include content placeholders that are already aligned on each slide, which eliminates the need for you to manually position things around or apply the right font or font colors. They also provide consistency when moving from one side to the next.

Here is an example of a PowerPoint Theme that has 14 slide layouts:

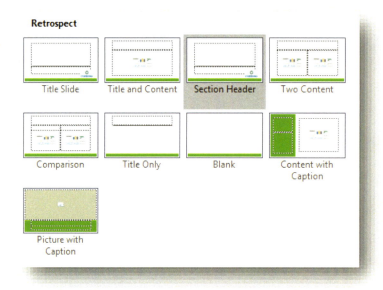

Figure 147. Standard Slide Layouts for a PowerPoint Theme

There are typically nine default layouts that come with most Microsoft PowerPoint Themes, but it will vary. Your company's Theme or template may have more or less depending on how customized it is. In my opinion, 15 layouts should be the maximum, since the first seven layouts will represent 90% of your slides. Let's take a look at the first seven layouts:

	Layout	Purpose
1	Title Slide	First slide of your presentation.
2	Title and Content	Basic slide layout (most overutilized).
3	Section Header	Layout to use for each new topic or new presenter (most underutilized).
4	Two Content	Perfect for two columns of content.
5	Comparison	Same as Two Content but includes placeholders for labels above the two columns of content.
6	Title Only	Use this layout when you want a blank canvas, perhaps for a full image or intricate diagram. Includes a title.
7	Blank	Use this layout when you want a blank canvas, perhaps for a full image or intricate diagram. It does not include a title.

To choose a slide layout while inserting a new slide

1. On the **HOME** tab in the **SLIDES** group, click the **NEW SLIDE** drop-down to view all the layouts available to you as seen in Figure 148.

Figure 148. New Slide drop-down to view available layouts

2. Select the most appropriate layout for the slide you are inserting.

To change a slide's layout to a different layout

1. Make sure you are viewing the slide that needs a different layout.
2. On the **HOME** tab in the **SLIDES** group, click the **LAYOUT** drop-down as seen in Figure 149 to view all the layouts available to you.

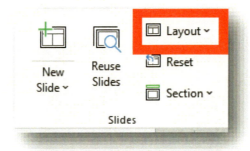

Figure 149. Layout drop-down to change existing layout to a different layout

3. Select the most appropriate layout for this slide.

Stop. If the fonts and font colors didn't adjust when you changed to a new layout, don't do anything manually! Be sure to check out the next tip, Tip #72 to instantly adjust the slide to the layout's settings.

This tip meets a MOS certification exam objective.

Tip #72   Fix a problem slide using the magical Reset button
Applies to all versions of Microsoft PowerPoint

The Reset button has to be the best kept secret in all of PowerPoint history! In my 20+ years of supporting PowerPoint users, 80-90% of them would have saved hours of time, reduced stress, and prevented missed deadlines having known about the Reset button.

For instance, suppose you accidentally nudged the slide's title out of position. Or someone changed the font on the slide to something other than what the font SHOULD be. Or you have a vast buffet of inconsistencies (colors, fonts, bullets). Rather than individually fix each item, click the Reset button to reset the slide to the defined Slide Layout. It's brilliant! No, it's magical.

You ready for this?

To fix a problem slide using the magical Rest button

1. On the **HOME** tab, in the **SLIDE** group, click **RESET** as seen in Figure 150 to reset the current slide to the definition of the layout.

Figure 150. The PowerPoint Reset Button

2. If it doesn't reset to the right layout, you may need to change the layout of the slide by going to the **HOME** tab, in the **SLIDE** group, click **LAYOUT** and apply the correct layout.
3. Once you've reset the slide to match the layout, you may need to make a few adjustments but thankfully, the fonts, bullets, colors and positioning of content should now be consistent with the other slides, or at least consistent with the Design Theme.
4. If the content doesn't go with the layout you've selected, then you may need to modify the layout itself, which is defined in the next Tip, or you can create a new layout as described in o.

Tip #73   Format multiple slides at once by modifying the layout

Applies to all versions of Microsoft PowerPoint

Let me ask you this. If you need to change the 1st level bullet style of all the slides in your presentation, would you rather (a) take the time and effort to change the bullets on each slide individually, or (b) make the change on one slide, which cascades down to all of the other slides that have bullets?

The obvious answer is (b), make the change on one slide. But most people don't approach it this way because they are unaware of this next tip: how to modify the layout in the slide master.

In this example, we'll change the bullet style for the first level bullet in our bulleted lists. If you want to change your fonts, see o.

Make a global change to your slides by modifying the slide master

1. On the **VIEW** tab, in the **MASTER VIEWS** group, click **SLIDE MASTER**. Now that you are in Slide Master view, notice all the layouts on the left-hand side of your screen. The screenshot below in Figure 151 shows the Slide Master

(#1) and its corresponding layouts. Not all the corresponding layouts have bullets. Those that do are identified in the screenshot by subsequent numbers.

Figure 151. Slide Master and corresponding layouts

In order to modify the first level bullet for all of the bulleted slides at once, you can simply make the change on the Slide Master (Slide #1), which will cascade down to any layout with bullets (Slide numbers 2-4). Any slides in your presentation using a bulleted list layout will then have the new bullet!

- Make sure you have selected the Slide Master slide (the top-level slide above all of the layouts).
- Click in the first bulleted line and on the **HOME** tab in the **PARAGRAPH** group, click the drop-down for the bullets. Choose a different bullet as seen in Figure 152.

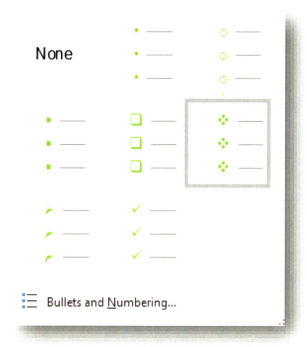

Figure 152. Changing bullets on our Slide Master

All the layouts with a bulleted list will now include this new bullet and as a result, all of the slides based on those layouts will now include the new bullet.

4. Close out of Slide Master view. On the **SLIDE MASTER** tab, in the **CLOSE** group, click **CLOSE MASTER VIEW**.
5. If one of your slides does not get updated with the new bullet, use the magical Reset button to reset it to the layout. See o if you need more help using the Reset button.

 This tip meets a MOS certification exam objective.

Tip #74 Create a new slide layout to reduce errors, ensure consistency, and save time

Applies to all versions of Microsoft PowerPoint

Slide layouts are a great tool to help you organize content on your slides consistently throughout your presentation. But what do you do when there isn't a slide layout to meet your needs?

© 2019 Vickie Sokol Evans, MCT The Red Cape Company, LLC. All Rights Reserved.

For instance, during monthly business reviews at a particular company, managers must include a slide with a chart, a table, and bulleted text to describe their business as seen in the example in Figure 153. Rather than insert each one of those items manually to slides and spend time aligning the objects on the slide, you can create a new slide layout to do most – actually, ALL – of the work for you.

Figure 153. Example custom slide layout for the team

In the above example, I need three Content placeholders. The placeholder on the left needs to be flexible. Employees can put any type of object on the left. But I need to force the team to always put their data table on the top right and their bulleted observations on the bottom right.

For planning purposes, here are the types of placeholders you can define on a layout:

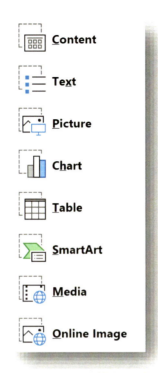

Figure 154. The 8 types of placeholders you can add to a slide

The Content placeholder gives you the MOST flexibility. The rest of them force you to only insert that type of object in that location on the slide.

To create a new slide layout

1. On the **View** tab, in the **Master Views** group, click **Slide Master**.
2. On the **Slide Master** tab, in the **Edit Master** group, click **Insert Layout** to insert a new slide.
3. To add placeholders, on the **Slide Master** tab, in the **Master Layout** group, click the drop-down arrow to the right of **Insert Placeholder** to view all the available placeholders as seen in Figure 155.

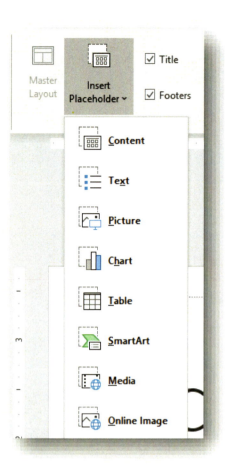

Figure 155. The Insert Placeholder drop-down menu

 I recommend using the Content placeholder to give your team flexibility when inserting their content. However, if you want to force your team to always insert the chart on the left and the table on the top right and text on the bottom right. Then, add those specific placeholders to the slide.

4. Once you know what type of placeholder you want, select the placeholder from the Insert Placeholder drop-down, which turns your mouse into a crosshair, and then draw the new placeholder on your slide in the preferred location.
5. Repeat Steps 3 and 4 for all the placeholders you wish to add to the new slide layout.
6. Rearrange and resize the placeholders, if necessary.
7. To rename your new layout slide:
    - Right-click the slide in the left pane of Slide Master view and select **RENAME LAYOUT**.
    - Give your layout a descriptive name and click **RENAME**.
8. On the **SLIDE MASTER** tab, in the **CLOSE** group, click **CLOSE MASTER VIEW**.

To insert a new slide using the new slide layout

1. On the **HOME** tab in the **SLIDES** group, click the **NEW SLIDE** drop-down arrow.
2. Select your new slide layout.

To apply the new slide layout to an existing slide

1. Navigate to the slide you wish to apply the new slide layout to.
2. On the **HOME** tab, in the **SLIDES** group, click the **LAYOUT** drop-down arrow.
3. Select your new slide layout.

This tip meets a MOS certification exam objective.

Be kind to your audience.

Tip #75 Convert boring text to SmartArt

Introduced in PowerPoint 2007

Tired of bulleted lists? Chances are, so is your audience! Make your ideas stand out by using SmartArt, which was first Introduced in Microsoft Office 2007.

SmartArt uses your existing bulleted list and magically converts them to a diagram or illustration that is much easier to organize and present.

Try it out, SmartArt is easy and fun!

To convert your text to SmartArt

1. Select the text you want to convert to SmartArt.
2. Right-click the selection and select **CONVERT TO SMARTART** to view a gallery of SmartArt graphics or on the **HOME** tab in the **PARAGRAPH** group, click **CONVERT TO SMARTART GRAPHIC** icon.

Figure 156. Convert to SmartArt

3. Select the graphic you want or click **MORE SMARTART GRAPHICS...** to view the entire library of SmartArt by category as seen in Figure 157.

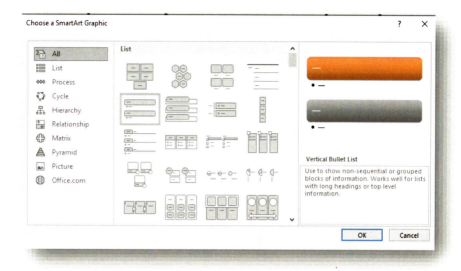

Figure 157. SmartArt Gallery

4. A separate dialog box pops up that allows you to easily add or rearrange the points on your slide.
5. Click the "X" in the top right-hand corner when you are finished editing the points.
6. To readjust the SmartArt points, open the Text pane by clicking the text handle on the left side of the SmartArt, as seen in Figure 158.

Figure 158. SmartArt Text handle

 This tip meets a MOS certification exam objective.

Tip #76 Add compelling transitions to your key topic slides
Applies to all versions of Microsoft PowerPoint

Adding transitions in your presentation visually guides your audience through the messaging and increases the effectiveness of your overall communication. In PowerPoint, you can add a different, more compelling transition for each of your main topics to visually cue your audience that you're moving to the next major point in your presentation.

In my presentations, my main topic slides are all defined as Section Header Layouts. And each of those slides are preceded by a Section, as seen in Tip #68. That way, the first slide in each section is a Section Header Layout. I usually apply a simple transition to all my slides and then go back and select each of the Section Header Layout slides and add a more compelling transition, such as Cube.

To add transitions to your key topic slides (Section Header Layouts)

1. Switch to Slide Sorter view. On the **VIEW** tab in the **PRESENTATION VIEWS** group, click **SLIDE SORTER**.
2. (Optional) To apply a simple transition for all your slides, select all by using [CTRL]+[A] and then click the **TRANSITION** tab; in the **TRANSITION TO THIS SLIDE** group select one of the transitions seen in Figure 159.

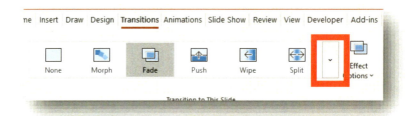

Figure 159. The More button in the Transition to This Slide group.

3. Now you need to make the first slide in each of your sections transition in a more compelling way. Click your first slide in the section. Typically, it will be the Section Header Layout slide. Hold down [CTRL] and click each of the Section Header Layout slides.
4. Once all your section header slides have been selected, add the compelling transition. On the **TRANSITIONS** tab in the in the **TRANSITION TO THIS SLIDE** group, select one of the transitions under the "Exciting" heading. You will have to either scroll through the list or click the **MORE** button below the Transition scroll bars as seen in Figure 159.

This tip meets a MOS certification exam objective.

Become an instant graphic artist.

Tip #77 Use picture tools to enhance your images

I've combined several Picture Tool tips from my previous books into one tip here. These include:

- Removing the background in an image
- Instantly styling your pictures
- Adding artistic effects

Introduced in PowerPoint 2007 and 2010

Remove the background in an image

Introduced in PowerPoint 2010

When adding images to a slide (or within an Excel or Word document for that matter) there will be times when you need to remove the background so that it is transparent. The Remove Background feature eliminates the need for a third-party tool such as a graphic design program to fix your picture.

1. Select the image in your presentation (or in your Excel or Word file).
2. On the **FORMAT** tab, in the **ADJUST** group, click **REMOVE BACKGROUND**.

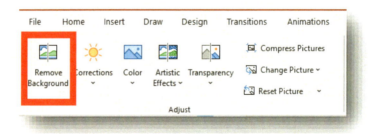

Figure 160. Remove Background button

3. Once you choose **REMOVE BACKGROUND**, your image will be outlined. Anything in magenta will be marked for removal. Use the handles on the outlined border to reposition the area of the image you want to keep, as seen in Figure 161.

Figure 161. Remove background feature

4. If an area you don't want to keep is NOT magenta, click the **Mark Areas to Remove** button on the **Background Removal** tab seen in Figure 162. Your cursor will change into a pencil. Use the pencil tool to draw a straight line through the area you want to remove as seen in Figure 163. Repeat for all areas you want to remove.

Figure 162. Remove Background Commands

© 2019 Vickie Sokol Evans, MCT The Red Cape Company, LLC. All Rights Reserved.

Figure 163. Draw a straight line through the area you want to remove.

5. If an area you WANT to keep is magenta, click the **Mark Areas to Keep** button on the **Background Removal** tab. Your cursor will change into a pencil. Use the pencil tool to draw a straight line through the area you want to keep as seen in Figure 164. Repeat for all areas you want to keep.

Figure 164. Draw a straight line through the area you want to keep

6. When you are done, click the **Keep Changes** button on the **Background Removal** tab.

This tip meets a MOS certification exam objective.

To style your pictures instantly

Introduced in PowerPoint 2007

Picture styles give your blah, flat images a professional look with the press of a button.

1. Select an image in your presentation. Notice the **PICTURE TOOLS** contextual tabs on the ribbon.
2. On the **FORMAT** tab in the **PICTURE STYLES** group, hover over one of the picture styles to see a preview of the style. Scroll through the list or click the **MORE** button below the **PICTURE STYLES** scroll bars seen in Figure 165.

Figure 165. The "More" button in the Picture Styles group

To add artistic effects to your images

Introduced in PowerPoint 2010

This is the coolest feature yet! Like photo filters on your smartphone's camera app, you can apply various artistic effects to your images in PowerPoint, Excel, Word, and Outlook.

1. Select your image. Notice the **PICTURE TOOLS** contextual tabs on the ribbon.
2. On the Picture Tools **FORMAT** tab, in the **ADJUST** group, select **ARTISTIC EFFECTS** to view the various effects that you can apply to your image.
3. Hover over each one to see a preview of what your image will look like.
4. When you're ready, select the one you like.
5. If you want to remove the effect from your image, on the Picture Tools **FORMAT** tab, in the **ADJUST** group, select **ARTISTIC EFFECTS** and choose the first image on the top left which is None.

Tip #78 Magically replace an image without affecting other objects and settings

Applies to all versions of Microsoft PowerPoint

You've spent a good 10 minutes getting an image in the right spot, with text across the image, hyperlinks and other objects only to realize that you need to switch out the background image without affecting the other objects on top of it.

Whatever you do, do NOT use the **INSERT PICTURE** feature. That's the long way! Instead, use the **CHANGE PICTURE** tool to do all the work for you.

To magically replace an image without affecting other settings

1. Right-click the image you want to replace.
2. Select **CHANGE PICTURE**.
3. Navigate to the new picture you want to use.
4. When you see the image, double-click the image to replace the old one. Note: the old one will be deleted from your slide or document and the new image will be now be in its place!

==This tip meets a MOS certification exam objective.==

Tip #79 Work with objects like the pros

Applies to all versions of Microsoft PowerPoint

I've combined several graphic design tips from my previous book into one tip here.

To draw straight lines

I can't draw a straight line, even square, or perfect circle to save my life. Luckily, my life doesn't depend on it. But if it did, I'd be safe because of the amazing [SHIFT] key!

1. On the **INSERT** tab in the **ILLUSTRATIONS** group, select **SHAPES** and click the line you wish to draw.
2. Hold down [SHIFT] as you draw the line and you'll never have a crooked line.

176 © 2019 Vickie Sokol Evans, MCT The Red Cape Company. All Rights Reserved.

To draw perfect squares and circles

1. On the **INSERT** tab, in the **ILLUSTRATIONS** group, select **SHAPES** and click the rectangle or oval shape.
2. Hold down the [SHIFT] key as you draw the rectangle or oval and the shape snaps into a perfect square or circle.

To dynamically connect two shapes together using a line or arrow

When you need to draw a connecting line between two shapes, you want to be sure that the line is attached to the shapes. That way, when you move either shape the line moves with it.

1. On the **INSERT** tab, in the **ILLUSTRATIONS** group, select **SHAPES** and click the line you wish to draw.
2. Hover over the first shape's handle to find the dots at each "target" handle for the shape and then choose one to start the line. Click, holding the mouse down and drag from that target handle to the other shape's target handle.
3. When you let the mouse go, the two shapes are connected with the line and two green dots show the connection points of the two shapes, as seen in Figure 166.

Figure 166. Dynamic Connection of Shapes

In PowerPoint 2010 and earlier versions, the connector dots are red instead of green.

This tip meets a MOS certification exam objective.

Tip #80   Use the new Designer tool to transform a slide

Introduced in PowerPoint 2016

I'm not a graphic designer, but the cool new Designer tool in PowerPoint 2016 makes me look like one!

When you insert an image onto a slide, the Designer tool is activated and presents about a half-dozen design ideas using the image. If it doesn't automatically activate, then you can activate the Designer tool whenever you want. Here's how:

To use the new Designer tool to transform a slide

1. Insert an image onto your slide.
2. If the Designer tool's "Design Ideas" pane doesn't launch automatically, then go to the **DESIGN** tab in the **DESIGNER** group and click **DESIGN IDEAS** to see options for your slide as seen in Figure 167.

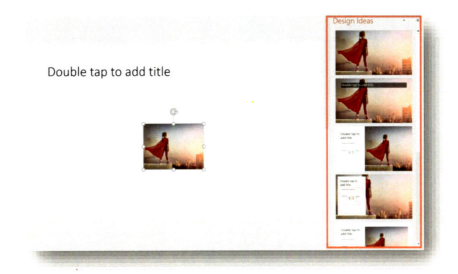

Figure 167. Design Ideas for the new image on a slide

3. Using the blank presentation PowerPoint template, I decided on this design:

Figure 168. Example design idea using the Designer Tool

 For more information about this feature, go to support.office.com and search for **PowerPoint Designer** and select: "Create professional slide layouts with PowerPoint Designer."

Present like the pros.

Tip #81   Use keyboard shortcuts to run your slide show
Applies to all versions of Microsoft PowerPoint

To run your slide show from the beginning using a keyboard shortcut

No matter what slide you're on in your presentation, you're one keystroke away from launching your presentation slideshow from the very beginning.

- Press the [F5] key from anywhere in your presentation.

To run your slide show from the current slide using a keyboard shortcut

- Navigate to the slide you wish to start from and press [SHIFT]+[F5].

Tip #82   See your notes and next slides while you are presenting
Applies to all versions of Microsoft PowerPoint

While your audience sees only your slides, Presenter View gives you a view of your notes and upcoming slides when you are making a presentation. If you practice using Presenter View before the big presentation day arrives, you'll be ready to impress with a production that is well-organized and effective.

Presenter View has been around for a while, but there are some major improvements in PowerPoint 2013. Not only does the interface look dramatically different, but also the new update eliminated the need you no longer have to connect to a projector or second monitor to work in Presenter View. It's great!

Switch to Presenter View

- When you connect a projector or another monitor, there is no set up required. Simply run the Slide Show using [F5] or [SHIFT]+[F5] as described in Tip #81.
- If you are NOT connected to a projector or another monitor, run the Slide Show on your screen and click the Control Bar (three dots) on the bottom

180   © 2019 Vickie Sokol Evans, MCT The Red Cape Company. All Rights Reserved.

left hand corner of your current slide and choose **Show Presenter View,** as seen in Figure 169.

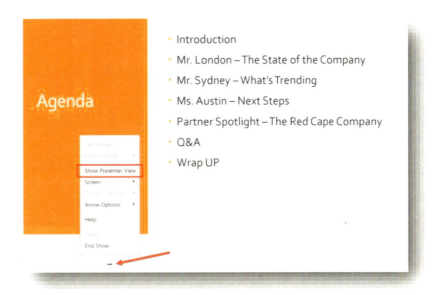

Figure 169. Show Presenter View during a slide show

Switch between Presenter View and Duplicate Screens

- When you need to revert to duplicate screens again, use the **Display Settings** option at the top of the Presenter View and choose **Duplicate Slide Shows**. However, this only works when you connect to a projector or second monitor.
- If you have only one monitor, click the **Presenter View Options** button and choose **Hide Presenter View**.

Figure 170. Presenter View options within Presenter View

Use Presenter View tools – available at the bottom of the screen

- Move through slides using the arrows shown in Figure 171.

Figure 171. Presenter View - Move through slides

- To point or write on slides, use the pencil icon shown in Figure 172.

Figure 172. Presenter View - Point or write on slides

- To view all slides (and sections, if any) in your presentation, click the **See all Slides** button shown in Figure 173.

Figure 173. Presenter View – See all slides (and Sections!)

- To zoom into a slide, use the magnifying glass shown in Figure 174.

Figure 174. Presenter View - Zoom into the slide

- To hide or unhide the current slide, click the **Black or unblack slide show** button shown in Figure 175.

Figure 175. Presenter View – Black or unblack slide show

- To see More Slide Show options, click the ellipsis (…) icon shown in Figure 176.

Figure 176. Presenter View - More slide show options

In PowerPoint 2010 and earlier editions, you must be connected to a second display such as a projector or a second monitor to use Presenter View. Once you have a second display connected, on the **SLIDE SHOW** tab, in the **MONITORS** group, check **USE PRESENTER VIEW**, then run your slide show: **SLIDE SHOW** tab > **START SLIDE SHOW** group > **FROM BEGINNING**. The interface is different than PowerPoint 2013, the many of the commands are available as seen in Figure 177.

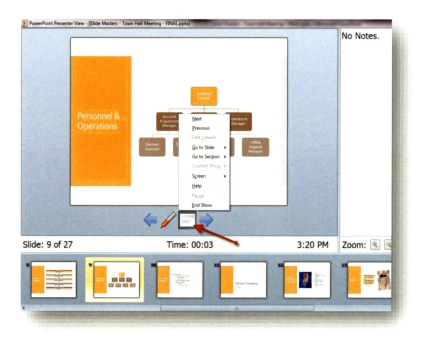

Figure 177. PowerPoint 2007/2010 Presenter View

Tip #83 Instantly and confidently jump to a slide or section while presenting

Applies to all versions of Microsoft PowerPoint

We've all been there: right in the middle of presenting a concept or answering an audience member's question, you realize that you need to show a specific slide to illustrate a point that you're trying to make. Or perhaps you need to resume your meeting at a specific location in your deck. Here's the best way for you to get to the slide or section that you need right away, without stumbling.

Jump to a slide or section during a presentation

1. If you haven't done so already, run the slide show by using [F5].
2. Right-click your current slide and select **SEE ALL SLIDES**.
3. Click the Section on the left to view all the slides in that section.
4. Then click the slide you need and you're ready to go!

In PowerPoint 2010 and earlier editions, right click a slide while you are presenting in Slide Show view and choose either **GO TO SLIDE** or **GO TO SECTION** and then the appropriate slide or section.

Tip #84 Zoom in on a slide

Introduced in PowerPoint 2013

Does your slide have detailed information that might be difficult for the folks in the back of the room to see? You're in luck! The new Zoom feature introduced in PowerPoint 2013 is the perfect tool for you to zoom in on important information that you won't want anyone to miss.

Zoom in on a slide while presenting

1. While presenting in slide show view, move your mouse to the bottom left hand side of the slide to see the Presenter tools available, as seen in Figure 178.

Figure 178. Slide show Zoom command

© 2019 Vickie Sokol Evans, MCT The Red Cape Company, LLC. All Rights Reserved.   185

2. Click the magnifying glass tool to get into Zoom mode and then click the area of the slide you want to zoom in on.
3. You can use the hand cursor to move around.
4. Once done, hit [ESC] to get out of Zoom mode.

Tip #85   Use recording tools to effectively communicate your message
Introduced in PowerPoint 2013

You don't need a separate third-party recording app to create tutorials for your team or customers. PowerPoint has you covered!

When a new person joins our team, we need to show him/her how to log into their Office 365 account to access their applications, OneNote notebooks, shared files and how to manage their account.

Additionally, we need to create short tutorials for our customers to showcase our offerings.

We can use PowerPoint to create the tutorials in breeze!

With the recordings, you can embed the videos into your PowerPoint slide deck or save as a separate video files to watch on demand.

First, let's examine the recording tools. I would suggest pinning the recording tools so you have them in view when you are recording.

Figure 179. PowerPoint recording tools

	Feature	Purpose
1	Record	Press the Record button when it's time to record.
2	Timer	Displays the time lapsed during the recording.
3	Select Area	Defines what part of your screen or presentation you want in the recording.
4	Audio	If you plan to record your voice, make sure this is turned on. Use your default sound recording devices to indicate which mic you want to use.

| 5 | Record Pointer | Keep this turned on if you are recording a tutorial of your screen and applications. Turn it off if you don't want your mouse to show up in the recording, perhaps when you are recording a presentation. |

To set your default mic for audio recordings

First, if you plan to record audio, make sure the mic you want to use is set as your default recording device:

1. Right-click the speaker in your Windows task bar and choose **RECORDING DEVICES**.
2. Select the microphone you want to use and then select **SET AS DEFAULT**.
3. Click **OK**.

Keep in mind while you are recording that you will only be able to trim the beginning and end of the video. You will not be able to trim out portions from the middle of the video. So take your time at the beginning before you say your first word and at the end when you've said your last word.

To record your desktop

Use this method to record what's happening on your screen perhaps for IT or for a colleague. Or you can record a process for new hires or your team.

1. In PowerPoint, insert a new slide where you want the recording to be placed even if it's temporary.
2. On the **INSERT** tab, in the **MEDIA** group, click **SCREEN RECORDING** to launch the PowerPoint recording tools as seen in Figure 179. Your screen will turn gray as it waits for you to select the area of your screen you want to record.
3. Click the **SELECT AREA** button on the Recording Tools and your mouse will turn to crosshairs that you can then use to draw the area you want to record.
4. Make sure all the websites, apps, and files you need during the tutorial are ready to go.
5. As I mentioned earlier, I would suggest pinning the recording tools so you have them in view when you are recording.
6. When you are ready, click the **RECORD** button.
7. Walk through the steps you want to demonstrate both on the computer and voice instructions. When you are finished, press [WINDOWS]+[SHIFT]+[Q] to stop the recording.

8. The recording will be inserted in the current PowerPoint presentation for playback. You can copy/paste the recording anywhere in this presentation or to another one.
9. To save it as a standalone recording, right-click the video and choose **Save Media As** and save it in a location of your choice with a new name.

To record your presentation

Use this method to record all or a portion of your presentation for on demand playback.

1. Insert a new slide where you want the recording to go on.
2. On the **Insert** tab, in the **Media** group, click **Screen Recording** to launch the PowerPoint recording tools as seen in Figure 179. Your screen will turn gray as it waits for you to select the area of your screen you want to record.
3. Put your presentation in Slide Show view.
4. Click the **Select Area** button on the Recording Tools and your mouse will turn to crosshairs that you can then use to draw the area you want to record.
5. If you don't want your mouse to show up while you are presenting your slides, turn off the **Record Pointer**.
6. As I mentioned earlier, I would suggest pinning the recording tools so you have them in view when you are recording.
7. When you are ready, click the **Record** button.
8. Walk through the slides you want to demonstrate both on the computer and voice instructions. When you are finished, press [WINDOWS]+[SHIFT]+[Q] to stop the recording.
9. The recording will be inserted in the current PowerPoint presentation for playback. You can copy/paste the recording anywhere in this presentation or another one.
10. To save it as a standalone recording, right-click the video and choose **Save Media As** and save it in a location of your choice with a new name.

To format and edit your video, click on the video on your PowerPoint slide to access the **Video Tools** > **Format** and **Playback** tabs.
OR

Right-click your video in PowerPoint to get two menus: the standard contextual menu plus a menu above it with three commands: **Style**, **Trim**, and **Start** as seen in Figure 180.

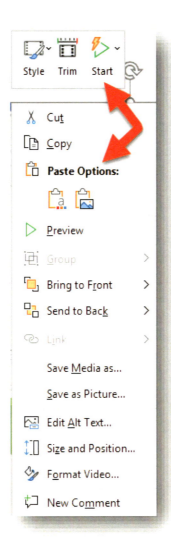

Figure 180. PowerPoint Video right-click menus

To set your video playback settings

1. Right-click your video in PowerPoint to access the video menu as seen in Figure 180.
2. Click **Start** to configure the video to start **Automatically** when the presenter (or viewer) advances to the slide or configure it to start **On Click** so that the video only starts when the person clicks the mouse to start it.

To style your video

1. Right-click your video in PowerPoint to access the video menu as seen in Figure 180.
2. Click **Style** to apply a cool look for the video frame.

© 2019 Vickie Sokol Evans, MCT The Red Cape Company, LLC. All Rights Reserved.

To trim your video

1. Right-click your video in PowerPoint to access the Video menu as seen in Figure 180.
2. Click **Trim** to launch the **Trim Video** window as seen in Figure 181.

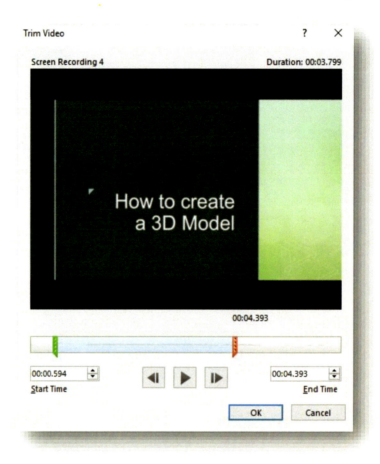

Figure 181. Trim Video window

3. To remove portions of the recording from the beginning, click the Play button to start the video.
4. When you reach the point where you want to the video to officially begin, click the Pause button. The green starting line indicated in Figure 181 marks the official start of the video where the cut will take place.
5. To trim the end of the clip, click the red ending point indicated in Figure 181 and drag it to the desired location where you want the video to end.
6. Click **OK**.

Chapter 6: Microsoft Outlook Tips

Reduce email volume, save time for yourself and others, find email fast, and automate your work.

In this Chapter

- Use timesaving features to process your email more effectively.
- Communicate more effectively with your team.
- Master digital etiquette tips that affect other people's productivity and angst.
- Master essential and effective search techniques.
- Automate manual processes and responses.

Reduce your email volume.

Tip #86   Instantly remove redundant messages using Clean Up

Introduced in Outlook 2010

Chances are, your mailbox has more messages in it than you'd like, and it can be overwhelming to see how many messages are sitting there awaiting your response or waiting to be moved or deleted. The good news is that many of those messages are redundant and can be quickly deleted with one press of a button.

What are redundant messages? Imagine you and I are sending messages back and forth about a project that we're working on together. For this one conversation, you received five messages from me and I received four messages from you. The last message I sent you contains the entire conversation, which means the other four messages from me are considered redundant. There isn't anything in those first four messages that isn't in the last message. Therefore, you can clean up our conversation by deleting the first four messages. But you're not going to do it manually. The Clean Up feature will do the work for you.

© 2019 Vickie Sokol Evans, MCT The Red Cape Company, LLC. All Rights Reserved.   191

Before I walk you through the Clean Up process, I need to point out a few things.

Attachments: If a message in a conversation has an attachment, it isn't considered redundant and therefore it won't be deleted. For instance, if the first message I sent you in a five-email conversation included an attachment, the Clean Up process would keep the email with the attachment (the first email), plus the last email (with the entire thread). It would only delete messages 2, 3 and 4.

Split Conversations: Additionally, if our conversation had multiple people on the thread and two people separately responded to the same email thereby creating a split conversation, those emails would not be considered redundant and would remain in your inbox or folder.

If the idea of letting Outlook automatically delete your email messages triggers anxiety, don't worry! There are plenty of ways the app protects your valuable information.

Other default redundancy settings:

- Don't move unread messages
- Don't move categorized messages
- Don't move flagged messages
- Don't move digitally signed messages
- When a reply modifies a message, don't move the original

Optional Setting: Before you begin using the Clean Up feature to delete redundant messages, I recommend that you create a Clean Up folder that you can refer to if you want to analyze what is being deleted. Otherwise, the messages will get moved to your Deleted Items folder by default.

Create a Clean Up folder and configure your Clean Up settings

1. On the **HOME** tab, in the **DELETE** group, click **CLEAN UP** as seen in Figure 182.

Figure 182. Clean Up button

2. Choose **CLEAN UP CONVERSATION** display in the Clean Up Folder dialog box. You will receive a popup message to confirm clean up, as seen in Figure 183.

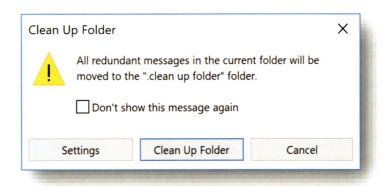

Figure 183. Clean Up folder confirmation

3. Click the **SETTINGS** button seen in Figure 183, which opens the Outlook Options dialog box seen in Figure 184.

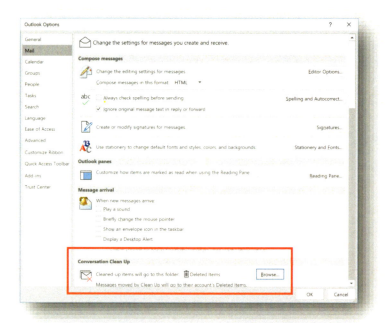

Figure 184. Clean Up folder - Outlook Options dialog box

4. Click the **BROWSE...** button and create a new folder as a subfolder of your Deleted Items folder, as seen in Figure 185.

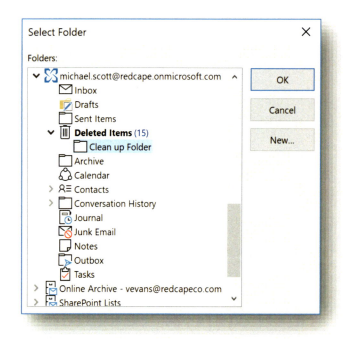

Figure 185. Clean Up Folder Settings - Select Folder

If your Deleted Items folder gets emptied every time you close Outlook, the new Clean Up folder may get deleted as well if you create it as a subfolder of your Deleted Items. In this case, you should consider creating a Clean Up folder as a subfolder of your Inbox instead.

5. Once you're done creating the Clean Up folder and saving it as the default folder, you should now be back at the Clean Up settings Folder confirmation seen in Figure 186.

Figure 186. Clean Up settings

6. (Optional) Confirm or change the sensitivity settings for redundant messages as seen in Figure 186.
7. Click **OK** to confirm settings.

Use Clean Up to quickly reduce your email volume

1. View your Inbox and jot down how many messages you currently have in your inbox so you can compare to the number of messages remaining in your Inbox after the Clean Up process.
2. On the **HOME** tab in the **DELETE** group, click **CLEAN UP** as seen in Figure 187.

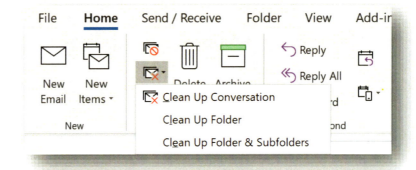

Figure 187. Clean Up button

You have three options:

- Clean up conversation – Only removes redundant messages in the conversation you have selected.
- Clean up folder – Removes redundant messages for the folder you are currently in, such as your inbox.
- Clean up folders and subfolders – Removes all redundant messages throughout your mailbox.

3. Choose **Clean Up Folder** to remove all redundant messages in your inbox. You will receive a pop up message to confirm clean up as seen in Figure 188.

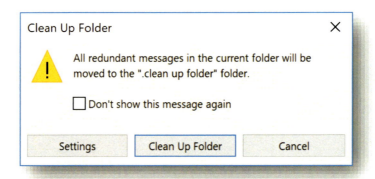

Figure 188. Clean Up folder confirmation

4. Click **Clean up Folder** to complete the action.
5. Next, take a look at the number of messages in your inbox and compare it to what you started with in Step 1. You can also navigate to your Clean Up folder that you created in Step 5 above and see how many redundant messages you had.

I recommend using the Clean Up button 2-3 times a day and choosing Folders and Subfolders. That way, you are constantly reducing your email volume and freeing up space.

 This tip meets a MOS certification exam objective.

Tip #87   Ignore conversations without hurting anyone's feelings
Introduced in Outlook 2010

One of the features introduced in Outlook 2010 is the Ignore button, which allows you to disregard an entire conversation without damaging any relationships.

When you Ignore a conversation in Outlook, related messages in the conversation are moved to the Deleted items. Additionally, any incoming messages for that conversation will automatically move to the Deleted items. This is one of the best and easiest ways to triage your mail in the mornings and throughout the day.

If you mistakenly ignored the wrong conversation thread, you can always remove the ignore command from the conversation and messages will appear back in your inbox.

To ignore an email conversation

1. Select one of the messages in the conversation.
2. On the **HOME** tab in the **DELETE** group, click the **IGNORE** button shown in Figure 189. All of the messages in that conversation will be moved to your Deleted Items.

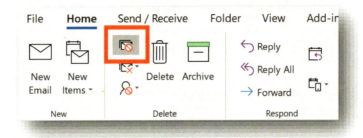

Figure 189. The Ignore button on the Home ribbon

To stop ignoring an email conversation

1. Go to your Deleted Items folder.
2. Select one of the messages in the thread that you ignored by mistake and click **IGNORE** again to turn it off. New messages will no longer be deleted automatically.

Tip #88   Reply with a meeting

Introduced in Outlook 2010

If you receive an email message from your manager or a customer asking to set up a meeting, you are one click away from getting it on everyone's calendar. Instead of bugging everyone to respond with their availability, you get the meeting set up in a jiffy and they will love how efficient you are!

Another benefit of the Reply with Meeting command is that it collectively reduces email volume for both you and the recipient(s) because you no longer have to go back and forth to set and confirm meetings. Plus, details from the email message will automatically be copied to your meeting request and anyone on the email thread will automatically be added as an attendee. Of course, you can always remove attendees and edit details during the meeting set up.

To reply with a meeting

1. On the **HOME** tab in the **RESPOND** group, click **MEETING**. Outlook will generate a meeting item and populate the following fields:
    - Meeting Subject = Email Subject
    - Meeting details = Email body
    - Meeting attendees = Email recipients and sender

Figure 190. Reply with Meeting button

2. Add the date, time, and location information.

Don't forget to set the correct date and time for the meeting! This is a common mistake.

3. Click. **SEND**.

Save time for yourself and others.

Tip #89   Reduce time zone errors

Applies to all versions of Microsoft Outlook

In today's global workplace, it's inevitable that you will set up meetings or conference calls for yourself and attendees in different time zones and you certainly don't want to make a mistake that causes someone to miss a meeting. Additionally, if you travel between time zones, you'll want to ensure that your flight gets added to your calendar correctly so that no matter where you are in the world, your calendar and your linked apps will always be correct. And you don't have to worry about Daylight Saving Time mishaps!

For my fellow nerds out there who want to know the back-end behavior of Outlook, here's what I found on Microsoft's website. "The start and end times for items in the Outlook Calendar are saved in the Coordinated Universal Time (UTC) format, an international time standard similar to Greenwich Mean Time. When you send a meeting request to an attendee in a different time zone, the meeting item is displayed at the respective local times on each person's calendar, but saved in UTC." Therefore, rather than convert the time zone in your head, which is risky behavior in my opinion, let Outlook and the servers do the work for you.

In this example, we'll walk through how to correctly add a flight that covers multiple time zones to your calendar. The flight leaves Houston (Central Time zone) and arrives in London (London's time zone). Your goal is to set the start time in Outlook as Central Time and the end time as London Time so that everything syncs beautifully.

When you land in a different time zone other than your local time zone, your mobile device will automatically adjust to the new time zone but your laptop will not. This means that when you open Outlook on your computer, you're viewing your calendar in your original time zone.

In order to change your laptop to the new local time zone, right-click on the date/time in the bottom right-hand corner of your computer screen. Click **ADJUST DATE AND TIME**. In your **DATE AND TIME** dialog box as seen in Figure 194 and Figure 195 depending on your version of Windows. Configure your settings as needed and click **OK**.

Reduce time zone errors

1. Create a new appointment on your calendar.
2. Enter the details for the title, date, and location.
3. If they aren't already turned on, display the Time Zone fields by clicking the Time Zones toggle to the right of the time fields, as seen in Figure 191.

Figure 191. Time Zones command in Outlook

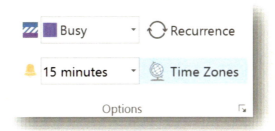

Figure 192. Time Zones command in the Outlook ribbon in previous version

4. Next, set the start and end time zones for the calendar item. If you're traveling across time zones, the start time zone will be different than the end time zone.
5. Make any necessary changes to the appointment and click SAVE & CLOSE.

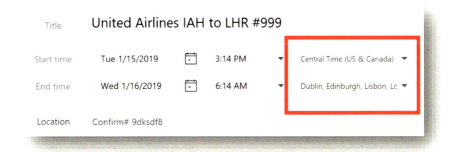

Figure 193. Time zones set for Houston (IAH airport) to London (LHR airport) flight

Figure 194. Date & Time setting for Windows 10

Figure 195. Windows Date and Time dialog box for previous versions of Windows

Tip #90   Create one-click links for mobile users

Applies to all email and calendar programs

When you view an email or details of an appointment on your smartphone, you've probably noticed by now that phone numbers and addresses are sometimes displayed as hyperlinks as seen in Figure 196. A hyperlinked address provides one-click access to navigation on your smartphone and a hyperlinked phone number provides one-click calling. It's not only convenient, it's safer for those who are driving and trying to find their way to that important meeting.

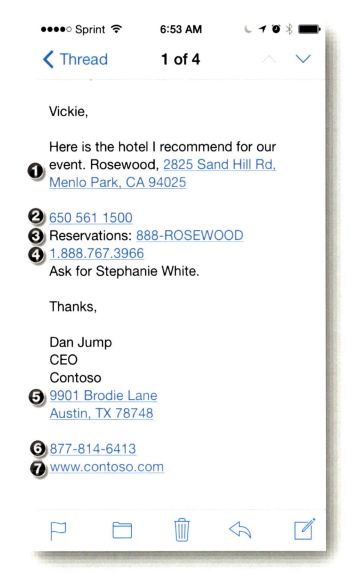

Figure 196. Active hyperlinks for phone and addresses on a mobile device

Let's take a closer look at what mobile users see when you either send them an email or store the details in a meeting request.

1. **Address on one line** – When you type an address on one single line versus as a block with line breaks, you still get the active hyperlink on the smartphone. Be careful though; if you include a building number or suite number, the hyperlink will break. Instead, put the building or suite number either before or after the address.

2. **Phone number with spaces** – This option should work just fine on most mobile devices. But test it out first! Send yourself an email with the phone number in the format of your choice and view and/or test the hyperlink on your phone to see if it works properly.

3. **Alphanumeric phone numbers** – Yay! The smartphone recognized an alphanumeric phone number. But beware, not all of the smartphones out there do so be sure to include the alternate numeric version along with the alphanumeric one just to be safe.

4. **Phone numbers formatted with periods** – The smartphone also recognized a phone number with periods instead of dashes.

5. **Address block** - When you type an address in standard block format, the hyperlink works great! Be careful though. If you include a building number or suite number anywhere in the address block, the hyperlink will break and it won't be correct. Your meeting attendees may get lost because the navigation won't work for broken links! Instead, put the building or suite number either before or after the address.

6. **Phone numbers formatted with dashes** – This option tends to work just fine as well, as all smartphones recognize dashes and will create the hyperlink correctly.

7. **Website** – As expected, this works just great on smartphones!

When addresses don't hyperlink. Take a look at Figure 197, which shows two versions of an appointment on a smartphone. Which one would you want to receive? Appointment A or B? It's the same address, but appointment B has a hyperlink that when clicked, will launch the GPS navigation app on your device. The reason why Appointment A doesn't have a hyperlink, is because the "raw" address is broken up and mixed in with floor, room, and cross streets. If 100 people were driving to this meeting, all 100 people would have to type the address into their GPS navigation app.

To ensure that the address always has a hyperlink, put building, suite, floor, and cross street information before or after the raw address. And always include a postal code! Even if you're texting or emailing your own address.

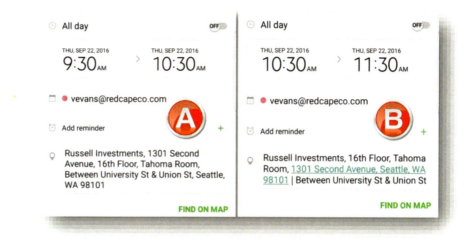

Figure 197. Compare address formats on recipient's smartphone

Create one-click links into a conference call

A member of my audience shared this next tip with me and I've been spreading the word about it ever since. I love connecting with people after RedCape events, so don't be shy!

When you or your manager needs to connect to a conference bridge while you are away from your desk – perhaps you're driving, in another building, or in some other remote place – you can obviously use your smartphone to dial the number. However, the device won't autodial the participant or host passcode for you. This means that you will have to write the passcode down before you make the call so that you can dial it in when prompted – which can be a huge hassle when you're on the move.

An easier and more convenient way – not to mention, cooler – is to create a hyperlink that will not only dial the conference call number but the participant or host passcode for you, too! Cool, right? Who doesn't want one-click entry into a conference call?

In our example, the conference call number is 877-814-6413. The participant passcode is 9374302, and then #. The one-click format will look like this:

1-877-814-6413,,,9374302#

Each comma represents a 1-second pause so the three commas in the example above represents a pause of three seconds.

6. Create a new meeting or modify and existing one.
7. In the location field, type your standard conference call info.
8. In the Meeting Notes field, type the following phrase: **1-Click Call-In for Mobile Devices:**

9. And then type the conference call number, three commas and the participant passcode. No need to include spaces.

10. Optional. If employees traditionally need to use the pound or hash key when dialing in, then add the pound or hash to the end of the passcode. So it should look like this: 1-Click Call-In for Mobile Devices: 1-877-814-6413,,,9374302#

Tip #91   Effortlessly work with attachments

Introduced in Outlook 2016

The attachments feature is one of the coolest new things available in Outlook 2016 is. Not only does Outlook show you the most recent item(s) you've been working on – for those of us using Office 365, Outlook also gives you the ability to attach a copy of the file or link to the file! Let's take a look at these two attachment features:

Attach a file from Recent Items

Suppose you are working on a proposal, report or contact list throughout the morning. The file is saved somewhere brilliantly in a folder, sub-folder, or sub sub-folder. Now, you need to send a copy of the file to a colleague – but where did you put it? Thankfully, you don't have to remember where you saved it. Outlook will show it in the list of **Recent Items** when you click **ATTACH FILE**, as seen in Figure 198.

1. Compose your message in Outlook.
2. On the **MESSAGE** tab in the **INSERT** group, click the **ATTACH FILE** drop-down to view your Recent Items list of documents no matter where you saved it on your system or in your cloud drives.

206   © 2019 Vickie Sokol Evans, MCT The Red Cape Company. All Rights Reserved.

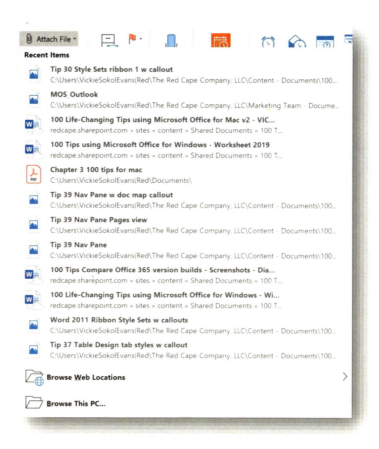

Figure 198. Recent Items list for Outlook attachments

Insert a static or dynamic attachment

If you know me personally, I'm a huge fan of sending links to documents versus attachments when I need my team to work together in the same document. The benefits of sending a link are:

- Reduces back and forth editing.
- Everyone always has the latest version.
- If you need to make a change to the original document after you've emailed the link, you can!

Although, when you're later searching Outlook for an email with a specific file attachment, there is a high probability you won't find it because the sender sent you a link to the document. Fortunately, Outlook 2016 has solved the problem with new dynamic and static attachments! **Note: you must be using Office 365 for this to work.**

1. Attach a file to an email in Outlook 2016. If the file is in a shared Office 365 drive such as OneDrive, SharePoint, Group, or Team file share, you will be

prompted to either share a link to the file or attach a copy of it, as seen in Figure 199.

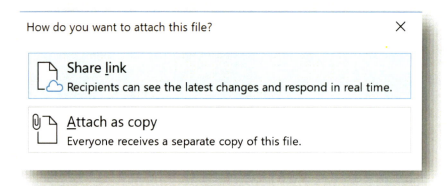

Figure 199. Attachment status for Office 365 attachments

2. If you are sending outside your organization or if you don't want your colleagues to have the latest and greatest version of the attachment, then select the option **ATTACH AS COPY** to turn it into a static copy.
3. To keep it a dynamic attachment that allows recipients or people within your organization to always access the latest and greatest version of the file, you can set permissions directly in Outlook. To do this, choose **SHARE LINK** and then click the drop-down arrow with options for the link attachment, as seen in Figure 200.

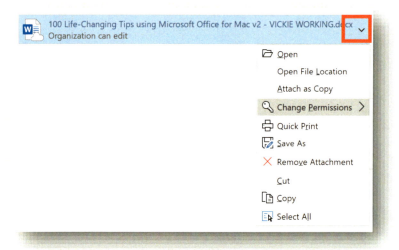

Figure 200. Attachments options for link attachments

4. To confirm or change permissions for the link attachment, select **CHANGE PERMISSIONS** as seen in Figure 201 and select which permission level you want from the submenu.

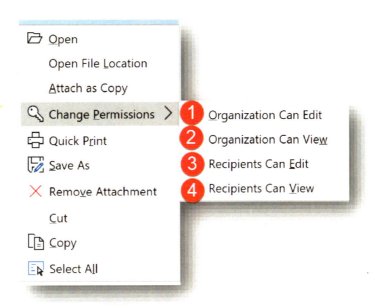

Figure 201. Permission options for link attachments

	Permission	Select this when
1	Organization Can Edit	It's okay for anyone in your organization to view/edit the file.
2	Organization Can View	It's okay for anyone in your organization to view the file but they cannot edit it.
3	Recipients Can Edit	Only the recipient(s) can view/edit the file.
4	Recipients Can View	Only recipient(s) can view the file, but they cannot edit the file.

Rule of thumb: Make life easier and save time by sending links to files instead of attachments, when possible. Outlook makes it so incredibly easy for those of us with Office 365!

This tip meets a MOS certification exam objective.

Tip #92   Use @mentions to improve communication and save time

Introduced in Outlook 2016

We're so strapped for time these days! It seems like there is so much email and noise vying for our attention, wouldn't it be nice to be laser-focused on only what's relevant among all the communication we receive via email?

Well, now there is! Using @Mentions in Outlook (and across Office 365) not only allows recipients to focus on their action items in a message or appointment, but it also gives you the ability to find Outlook items that specifically mention you.

Use @mentions when drafting an email

1. Type the **@** and then type your colleague's name or customer's name. Outlook will do its best to complete the mention with their username.
2. Then type out the action item or message for that person. For instance: **@Angela Martin: How much do we spend on office supplies each month on average?**
3. Complete the message and send.

Search for relevant email and action items using your @mention

1. At the top of your Inbox, you will see filters for All, Unread, and Mentions, as seen in Figure 202.

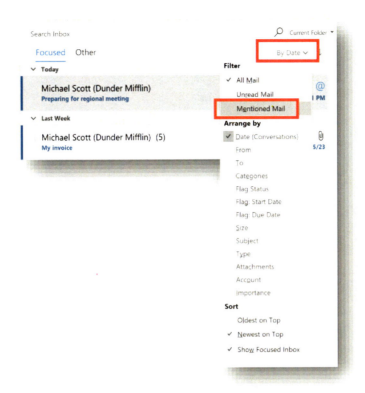

Figure 202. Inbox filters for Outlook > filter for Mentioned Mail

2. Click the **MENTIONED MAIL** filter to view all email in the current folder that mentions you. Then view each email with your @mention so that you can act or respond accordingly. For instance, Angela Martin and Pam Beesly are @mentioned in the email in Figure 203.

Figure 203. Recipient's email with @Mentions

Tip #93 Avoid embarrassing mistakes when repurposing and resending messages

Applies to all versions of Microsoft Outlook

I'm a huge fan of repurposing content to save time. I mean, who wants to reinvent the wheel?!

There are two common scenarios for repurposing content in Outlook: (a) copying/pasting content and (b) resending messages. Let's look at each scenario and the risks for each one:

- **Copying/pasting content from various sources** – Use this method when you are composing an email that includes supporting information collected from the web, your company's intranet, documents, or other emails.
The Risk: You will most likely end up with a mixture of fonts, colors, hyperlinks, and formatting, sometimes unbeknownst to you but very apparent to the recipient. This can look unprofessional, as seen in Figure 204.
The Solution: Use the Clear Formats button to reset formatting so that everything looks cohesive.

Figure 204. Example of mixed formats when repurposing content

- **Resending a message** – Use this method when you want to send the same email to more than one person and personalize each one. You can also use this method if the email bounced back because of a wrong email address.
The Risk: most people mistakenly use the Forward button in Outlook to resend a message, as seen in Figure 205, resulting in (1) extra steps to remove the FW in the subject and (2) formatting/color issues with the text, which again, affects the quality of the email and your professional brand.
The Solution: Use the Resend Message button instead of the Forward button.

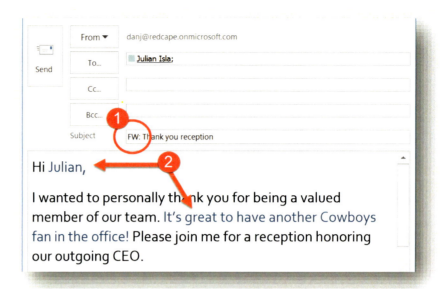

Figure 205. Bad example of resending a message.

To clear and reset all formatting when repurposing content

1. Compose your message in Outlook by copying and pasting content from various sources. Don't worry if the formatting doesn't match - we'll fix it!
2. Select all the content in your message that you want to reset the formatting for (excluding your signature).
3. On the **MESSAGE** tab, in the **BASIC TEXT** group, click the **CLEAR ALL FORMATTING** button seen in Figure 206. The text will reset to the default formatting for that message type. For instance, if it's a new message, the font color will be black. If it's a reply or forward, it will be blue text. All hyperlinks will be blue.

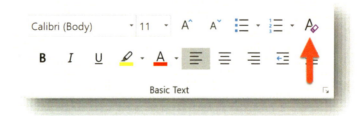

Figure 206. Clear All Formatting button.

To resend a message to a different person

When you want to send the same message to anther recipient, you can do so in Outlook using the Resend command. This feature allows you to personalize a previously-sent email to someone else. You can also use this feature to resend a message that bounced back!

1. Navigate to your Sent Items folder and double-click the message you want to resend.
2. On the **Message** tab in the **Move** group, click the **Actions** button and then select **Resend this Message,** as seen in Figure 207.

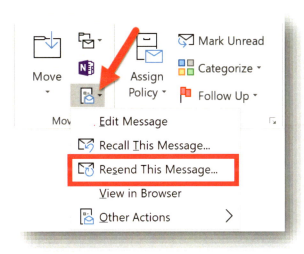

Figure 207. The Resend command on the Actions drop-down menu

3. Delete the previous recipient from the message and add the new recipient.
4. Make any necessary changes to the content of the message.
5. When you have completed your changes, click **Send** and then close the original message.

Tip #94 Use fancy email options to set your mail to expire and redirect replies

Applies to all versions of Microsoft Outlook

There are two really cool email options that have been around a long time but are definitely underutilized:

- Email expiration
- Direct replies to

Set the expiration date and time for a message

This tip might help you get nominated for coworker of the month!

Be kind to your colleagues and set expiration dates for timely emails. Messages that expire will display in the recipient's inbox as "crossed off" giving recipients an important visual cue that the message is no longer relevant, as seen in Figure 208. This allows your colleagues to stay focused on what matters most.

Figure 208. Expired message from Karen Berg sitting in an Inbox

1. Compose your email message.
2. On the **OPTIONS** tab in the **MORE OPTIONS** group, click the dialog box launcher button as seen in Figure 209. This launches the **PROPERTIES** dialog box.

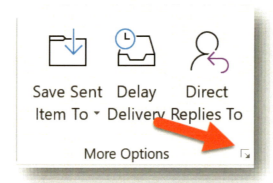

Figure 209. Dialog box launcher for More Options

3. Click the **EXPIRES AFTER** check box and type in the specific date and time that the message expires, as seen in Figure 210.

Figure 210. Expires After setting for messages

4. Click **Close**.
5. Click **Send** when you're done drafting your message. You won't see any difference on your end but your recipient's will when the message expires, and they will be your biggest fan!

Redirect replies to another team member

Imagine this: you are a manager drafting a very important email to the team that will guarantee responses. But you need another team member to manage the responses to ensure a high level of service. While the email comes from you, you can set up Outlook to redirect any and all replies to another person or mailbox!

1. Compose your email message.
2. On the **Options** tab in the **More Options** group, click **Direct Replies To** to launch the **Properties** dialog box as seen in Figure 211.

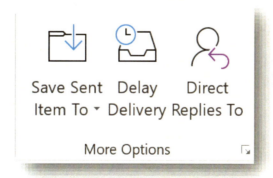

Figure 211. Direct Replies To command on the Ribbon

3. Click the **Have replies sent to** check box and type in the mailbox replies should be redirected to, as seen in Figure 212.

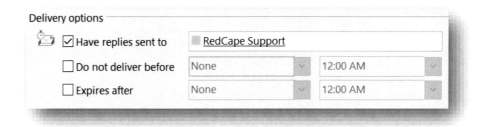

Figure 212. Have Replies Sent To option

4. Click **CLOSE**.
5. Click **SEND** when you're done drafting your message. When anyone replies to your message, the reply will be automatically sent to the other mailbox and the recipient will be aware of that.

Find email fast.

Tip #95 Quickly search for email using the powerful Search Bar

Introduced in Outlook 2010

It can be a daunting task searching for the email or attachment you need. On numerous occasions, you've probably asked yourself, "What folder is that email in?" or "Where did that attachment go?"

Rather than question yourself, find what you're looking for in seconds by using the **Search** bar at the top of your Inbox. As seen in Figure 213, Outlook's **Search** feature includes "scope" that helps you expand or narrow your search throughout your mailbox, and "refinements" that allow you to select exactly what you're looking for.

Figure 213. Search Ribbon in Outlook

Search should be your go-to method for finding email, rather than sorting or going through folders. That's why Google is so popular. It relies on search, not folders! Treat Outlook like you would Google. Use the search function every chance you get.

Start by memorizing [CTRL]+[E]!!

[CTRL]+[E] activates it all.

To search for email using the Search Bar

1. While in your Inbox, click the **Search** field at the very top of your message list as seen in Figure 214. Alternatively, you can use the [CTRL]+[E] keyboard shortcut.

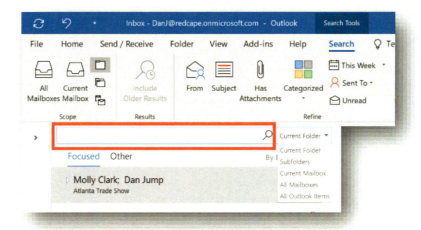

Figure 214. Outlook Search Bar

2. Once you click in the **SEARCH** field, it will activate the **SEARCH** ribbon seen in Figure 215.

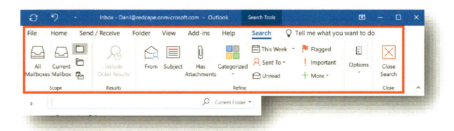

Figure 215. Outlook Search Ribbon

3. To change the scope to include all mailboxes, choose **ALL MAILBOXES**, from the **SCOPE** group in the ribbon or from the **SCOPE** drop-down list on the Search bar as seen in Figure 214, otherwise leave it on the default setting **CURRENT FOLDER**.
4. To search for a message from a person, click the **FROM** button, which places the proper search code in the Search field. Then type in the person's name or a partial email address.
5. To find only those messages that have attachments from that person, click **HAS ATTACHMENTS**.
6. Then hit [ENTER].

==This tip meets a MOS certification exam objective.==

220 © 2019 Vickie Sokol Evans, MCT The Red Cape Company. All Rights Reserved.

Tip #96   Create dynamic Search Folders to return to frequent searches

Introduced in Outlook 2007

Outlook Search Folders are dynamic folders you create and access to instantly display mail that meets specific criteria from your entire mailbox no matter where they are located. Examples of Search Folders you might have:

- **Unread mail** – All unread mail
- **To do for my manager** – All flagged mail (not completed) from Dan Jump
- **To do for clients** – All flagged mail (not completed) with Category = client
- **High priority mail** – All mail sent to me that is marked as high priority
- **High priority mail not completed** – All mail sent to me that is marked as high priority and flagged (not completed)
- **Mail sent only to me** – All mail where I'm in only person in the To: field
- **Project A** – All mail categorized as Project A
- **Project B** – All mail categorized as Project B
- **Event A** – All mail categorized as Event A
- **Event B** – All mail categorized as Event B
- **Large mail** – All mail larger than 5000 KB

The scope for these Search Folders is All Folders. This means that each one of these Search Folders will display mail no matter what physical folder they are in. And they will always show the latest and greatest emails – that's why they are considered dynamic!

Depending on your version of Outlook, you will have a couple of default Search Folders, such as those seen in Figure 216.

© 2019 Vickie Sokol Evans, MCT The Red Cape Company, LLC. All Rights Reserved.

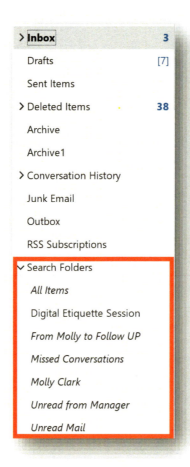

Figure 216. Default Search Folders in the Mailbox folder list

To create a "To Do for My Manager" Search Folder

1. View your email Folder List in Outlook, as seen in Figure 216.
2. Right-click **Search Folders** and choose **Create Search Folder**.
3. Scroll down to find the **Custom** category and choose **Create a custom Search Folder** seen in Figure 217.

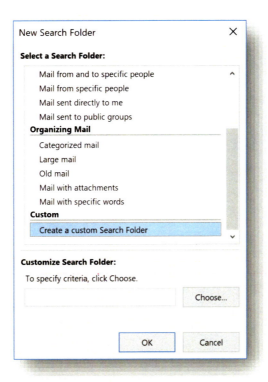

Figure 217. New Search Folder

4. Under the **CUSTOMIZE SEARCH FOLDER:** heading, click the **CHOOSE…** button to launch the **CUSTOM SEARCH FOLDER** dialog box shown in Figure 218.

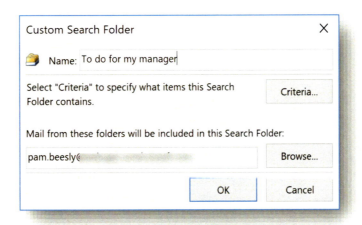

Figure 218. Custom Search Folder dialog box

5. Name the search folder **To Do for My Manager** or whatever you'd like to name it.
6. Click the **CRITERIA…** button.
7. On the **MESSAGES** tab, click the **FROM…** button to begin the search for your manager as seen in Figure 219.

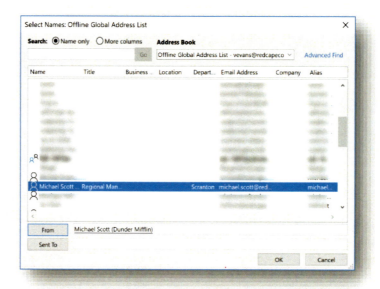

Figure 219. Select Names dialog box for the Search Folder

8. Click **OK,** and your manager's name will show up in the **FROM** field as seen in Figure 220.

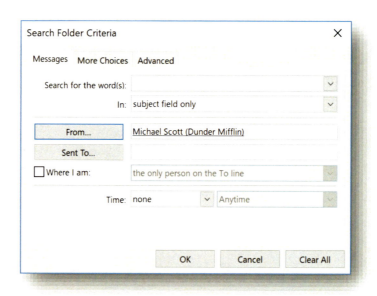

Figure 220. The "From" setting for Search Folders

9. Click the **MORE CHOICES** tab.
10. Select **ONLY ITEMS WHICH** and set it to **ARE FLAGGED BY ME,** as seen in Figure 221.

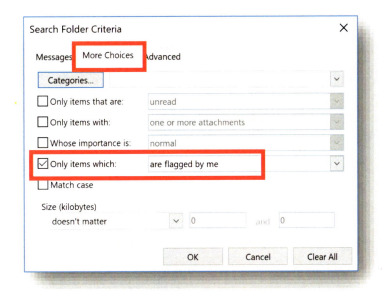

Figure 221. More Choices tab in the Search Folder Criteria dialog box

11. Click **Ok** to save the **Search Folder**.
12. To use the **Search Folder**, in your Folder List as seen in Figure 216, expand **Search Folders** and click **To Do for My Manager** to find all messages from your manager that are flagged by you.
13. Once you complete your manager's request, mark the email as complete or clear the flag and the email will no longer show up in the search results.

 This tip meets a MOS certification exam objective.

Automate your work.

Tip #97 Use conditional formatting to highlight messages from VIPs
Applies to all versions of Microsoft Outlook

One really cool way to automate your work is to apply conditional formatting to messages in your Inbox, such as highlighting all messages from your manager. That way, that you can easily see important messages because they stand out among all the other stuff in your inbox.

To add conditional formatting to your inbox

1. On the **VIEW** tab in the **CURRENT VIEW** group, click **VIEW SETTINGS**.
2. Click **CONDITIONAL FORMATTING**.
3. Click **ADD**.
4. In the **NAME** field, enter your manager's name, your biggest client's name, or anyone else you consider a VIP.
5. Click the **FONT** button and choose the formatting you want applied to his/her emails in your inbox. In my example, I chose Purple color, Trebuchet font, and Size = Big as seen in Figure 222. Click **OK**.

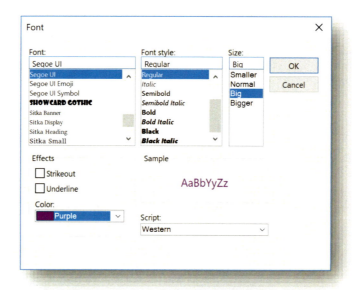

Figure 222. Outlook conditional formatting font dialog box

6. Once you've accepted the Font settings, you'll now need to set the condition. Click the **CONDITION** button seen in Figure 223 to launch the **FILTER** dialog box.

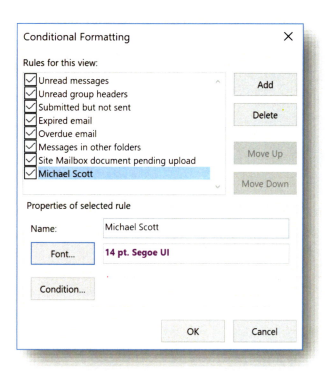

Figure 223. Conditional Formatting dialog box in Outlook

7. In the **FILTER** dialog box, click the **FROM** button to launch the **SELECT NAMES** dialog box.
8. Search for your manager's name and make sure that the **FROM ->** button at the bottom of the dialog box displays your manager's name, as seen in Figure 224.

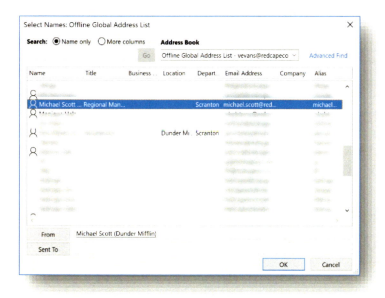

Figure 224. Select Names dialog box

9. Click **OK**.
10. The filter settings for your conditional format will display your manager's name in the **FROM** setting, as seen in Figure 225.

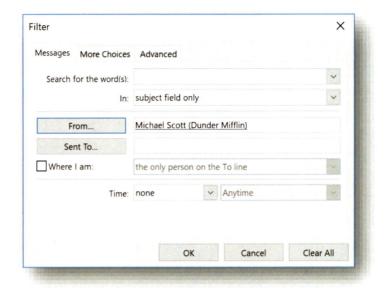

Figure 225. Filter Settings for the Conditional Format

11. Click **OK** to get back to the **CONDITIONAL FORMATTING** dialog box.
12. Click **OK** to return to the **ADVANCED VIEW SETTINGS** dialog box.
13. Click **OK** to return to your Inbox, which should now display messages from your manager in purple, as seen in Figure 226.

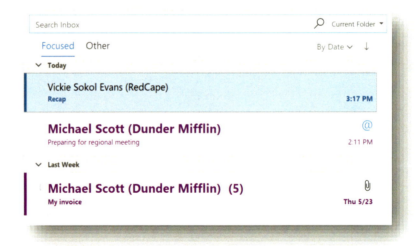

Figure 226. Conditional formatting applied to Michael Scott's emails

To edit Conditional Formatting

1. On the **VIEW** tab in the **CURRENT VIEW** group, click **VIEW SETTINGS**.

2. Click **CONDITIONAL FORMATTING** to launch the **CONDITIONAL FORMATTING** dialog box seen in Figure 227.

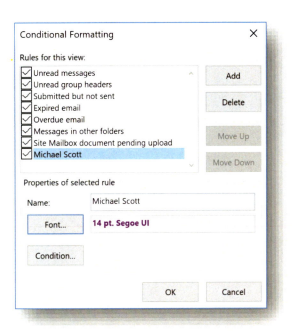

Figure 227. Conditional Formatting Rules

3. Select the rule you want to edit.
4. Click the **FONT** or **CONDITION** buttons to make changes to the rule.

Tip #98 Create rules to process and reroute messages
Applies to all versions of Microsoft Outlook

Another way you can automate your work in Outlook is to set up rules that will process and reroute messages for you. Examples of common rules include mail with any of the following conditions:

- From a specific person
- With a particular subject or message in the body
- Sent to you only
- Categorized
- Flagged
- Autoreplies
- Has attachments
- Meeting invites and much more!

© 2019 Vickie Sokol Evans, MCT The Red Cape Company, LLC. All Rights Reserved.

Rules by default work automatically, meaning that once you create them, they run in the background when the conditions of the rules are met. In this example, we'll create an automatic rule that categorizes all messages where I'm in only one in the **To:** field.

In this example, our ficticious employee Angela Martin will apply a "follow up today" flag on all mail sent only to her by her manager Michael Scott.

To create a rule flagging messages only sent to you by your manager

1. From your Inbox, go the **Home** tab. In the **Move** group, click the drop-down for **Rules** and choose **Create Rule**... to launch the **Create Rule** dialog box. Based on what email you selected, Outlook will pull in the sender and the subject from that message. In Figure 228, you can tell that an email from Michael Scott was selected when the process was initiated. All of these details can be modified if you didn't select a message from your manager.

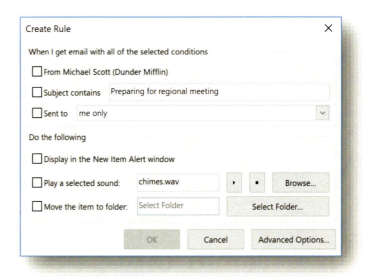

Figure 228. Create Rules dialog box

2. Click **Advanced Options** to open the **Rules Wizard** as seen in Figure 229.

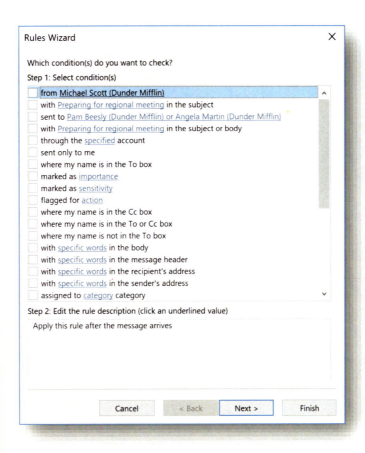

Figure 229. Create a rule using the Rules Wizard

- Select two conditions: **FROM** and **SENT ONLY TO ME,** as indicated in Step 1 of Figure 230. In Step 2, notice the conditions from Step 1 are pulled into the Step 2 of the Wizard. Pay attention to the hyperlinked **FROM** setting.

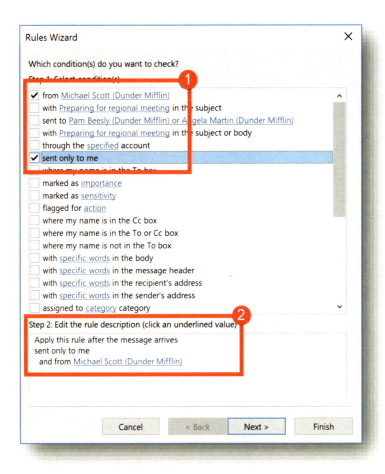

Figure 230. Rules Wizard Step 1

4. In Step 2, configure any hyperlinked conditions. If your manager's name isn't the hyperlinked condition like in our example, then click the hyperlink to change it to your manager's name and get back to the screen you see in Figure 230.
5. Click **Next**.
6. Now you'll configure the action. And in this example, we want to flag the message for follow up today. In Step 1 of the dialog box seen in Figure 231, select **Flag message for follow up at this time**.

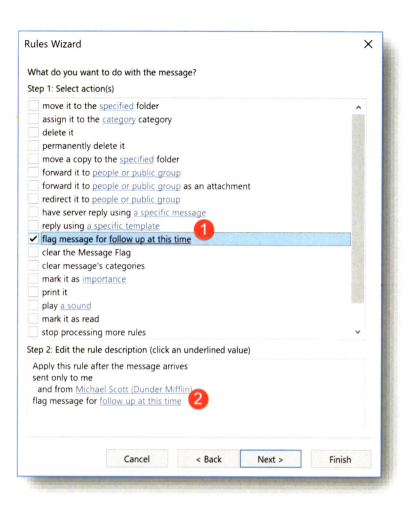

Figure 231. Rules Wizard set action

7. In Step 2, click the hyperlinked action to configure the follow up flag, as seen in Figure 232.

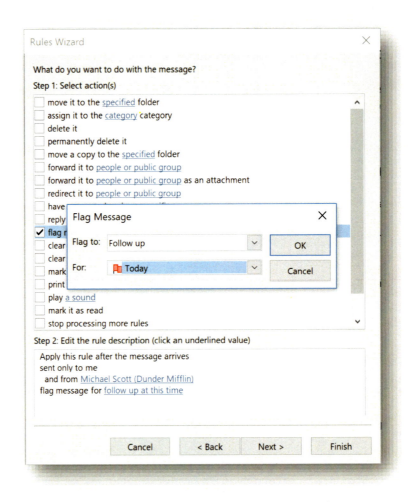

Figure 232. Setting the action to follow up today

8. Click **OK**.
9. Click **NEXT** to go to configure any Exceptions. We can skip this step.
10. Click **NEXT** to name your rule. In Step 1 of the setting, Angela will name it **Reply to Michael today** and in Step 2, she will select **RUN THIS RULE NOW…** as seen in Figure 233.

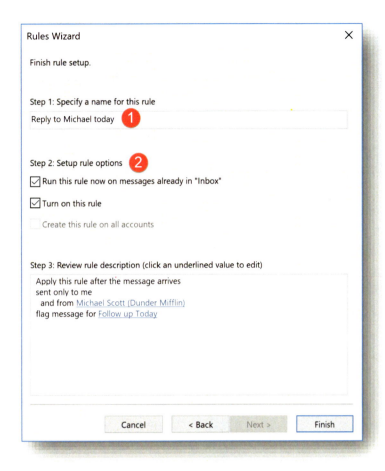

Figure 233. Final step of Rules Wizard

11. Click **Finish** to complete the rule setup.

 <mark>This tip meets a MOS certification exam objective.</mark>

Tip #99   Use Quick Steps to automate multi-step processes
Introduced in Outlook 2010

Quick Steps are easy-to-build shortcuts that give you one-click access to a repetitive multi-step process in Outlook. They are similar to macros, but so much easier to build and use! Examples of Quick Steps include:

- Creating and addressing an email to your immediate team in one click
- Creating and addressing an email to a project or ad-hoc team in one click

© 2019 Vickie Sokol Evans, MCT The Red Cape Company, LLC. All Rights Reserved.

- Repeatedly recreating a meeting with the same group of attendees and same call-in details
- Replying to a message and sending the original to the deleted items in one click
- Sending a boilerplate response to a vendor or colleague in one click
- ...and much more!

Ready to start dreaming of ways you can automate your work? Check out the list of over 25 actions you can configure into Quick Steps for yourself:

Full List of Quick Steps

Category	Steps Available
Filing	Move to Folder
	Copy to Folder
	Delete message
	Permanently delete message
Change Status	Mark as read
	Mark as unread
	Set importance
Categories, Tasks and Flags	Set retention policy
	Categorize message
	Clear Categories
	Flag Message
	Clear flags on message
	Mark complete
	Create a task with attachment
	Create a task with text of message
Respond	New Message
	Forward
	Reply
	Reply All
	Reply with Meeting
	Forward message as an attachment
Appointment	New Meeting

236   © 2019 Vickie Sokol Evans, MCT The Red Cape Company. All Rights Reserved.

Category	Steps Available
	Create an appointment with attachment
	Create an appointment with text of message
Conversations	Always move messages in this conversation
	Ignore messages in this conversation

Microsoft has started a handful of Quick Steps for you to configure:

Figure 234. Default Quick Steps

	Quick Step	Description
1	To Manager	Forwards the selected email to your manager. When you use this Quick Step for the first time you will be asked to configure it.
2	Team Email	Creates a new email to your team. When you use this Quick Step for the first time, you will be asked to configure it.
3	Done	Marks the selected email as complete, moves the email to a folder, and marks the email as read. When you use this Quick Step for the first time, you will be asked to configure it.
4	Reply & Delete	Replies to the sender and deletes the original email. No set up needed.
5	Create New	Create a new Quick Step from scratch
6	New Quick Step	Create a New Quick Step from a template:

Quick Step	Description
	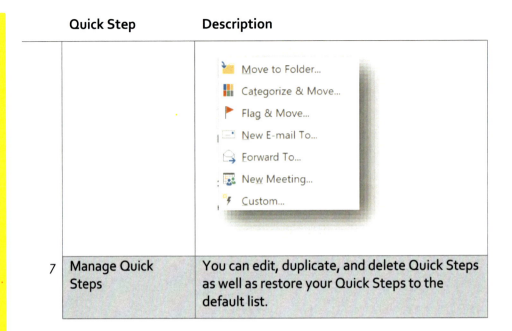
7 Manage Quick Steps	You can edit, duplicate, and delete Quick Steps as well as restore your Quick Steps to the default list.

Now that you know the basics, we are going to create two Quick Steps. The first Quick Step is to email your immediate team. The second Quick Step is to email a project or ad-hoc team.

To create and use a Quick Step to send a message to your team

1. In your Inbox, go to the **HOME** tab in the **QUICK STEPS** group and click **TEAM EMAIL**.
2. If you have already configured this button, a new message launches automatically addressed to your team. If not, you will be required to configure the Quick Step the first time you use it as seen in Figure 235.

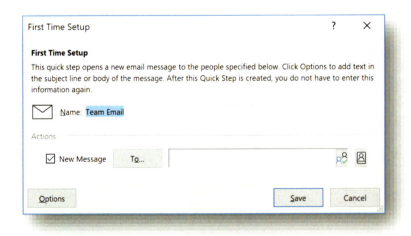

Figure 235. First Time Setup dialog box for Team Email Quick Step

3. In the FIRST TIME SETUP dialog box, rename the Quick Step, if necessary. For instance, **Email my team**.
4. Always click OPTIONS to view all the features available for this Quick Step, as seen in Figure 236.

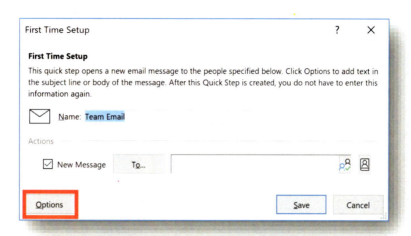

Figure 236. Click the Options button to configure your Quick Steps

5. Select your team members by clicking on the TO... button, then type each email address in the field. Use the Address book button to look up and confirm names, as seen in Figure 237.

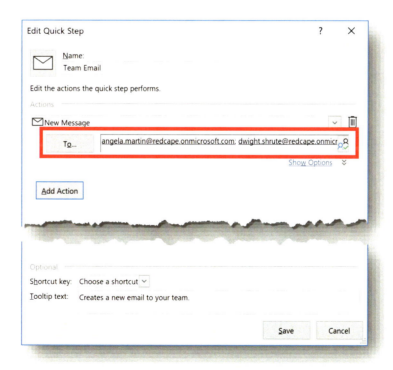

Figure 237. Email addresses added to the Team Email First Time Setup dialog box

© 2019 Vickie Sokol Evans, MCT The Red Cape Company, LLC. All Rights Reserved. 239

6. When configuring Email-specific actions, always click **SHOW OPTIONS,** as seen in Figure 238.

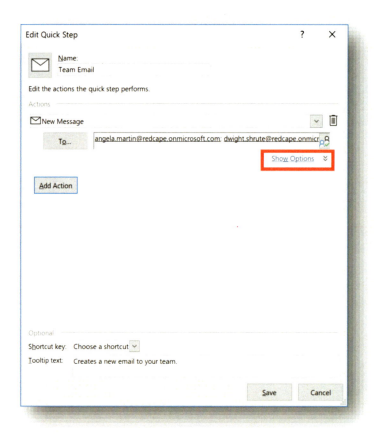

Figure 238. Edit Quick Step dialog box

7. Once you see the email options available in the **EDIT QUICK STEP** dialog box as seen in Figure 239, you can compose the boiler plate content.

- In the Text area type your standard greeting include some empty space for a custom message, and then add your internal signature.
- You can also add people to the CC and BCC lines if you always want them to be included.
- I recommend leaving the **SUBJECT** blank since that needs to be relevant to the message you are sending at the moment.
- I also recommend leaving the **FLAG** and **IMPORTANCE** settings as is so that you can turn those on when it's relevant to your message.
- Leave the **AUTOMATICALLY SEND AFTER 1 MINUTE DELAY** blank so that the message gets sent when *you* hit the **SEND** button.

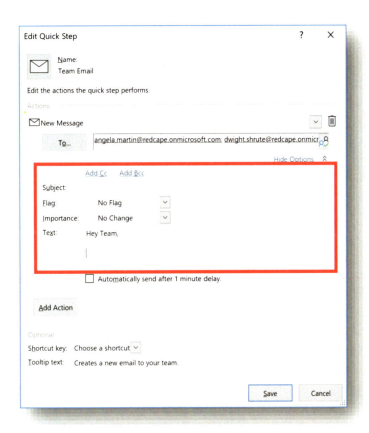

Figure 239. Edit Quick Step Email Options

8. When you are done configuring your **TEAM EMAIL** Quick Step, click **SAVE**.
9. To use the Quick Step, click on the Quick Step you just created, which will launch a new email message to the team.

 Once your Quick Step is configured, you can modify it by right-clicking the Quick Step and choosing **EDIT**.

To create and use a Quick Step to send a message to a project team

Let's create a Quick Step to send a message to a project team or an ad-hoc team. Think of a team you work with on a regular basis or for an upcoming project that may or may not be in the same department. For instance, when I worked at as a Business Analyst, there was a group of us Analysts that worked in different departments but regularly collaborated and mentored each other. In this example, I would create a Quick Step called **Email Analysts** and configure the email to include the other seven analysts in the **TO**: field, which would save me time when I needed to email the group.

1. In your Inbox, go to the **Home** tab in the **Quick Steps** group and click **New Quick Step**. Then, select **New Email to...** to launch the **First Time Setup** dialog box seen in Figure 235.

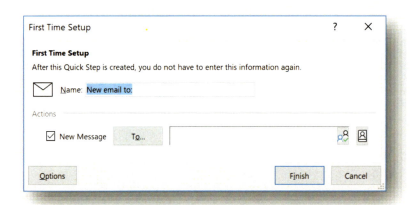

Figure 240. First Time Setup dialog box for Team Email Quick Step

2. In the **First Time Setup** dialog box, rename the Quick Step, if necessary. For instance, **Email Analysts**.
3. Follow the steps above beginning with Step 5 to complete the new Quick Step.

 This tip meets a MOS certification exam objective.

Tip #100 Create automatic responses and links to websites using Quick Parts

Introduced in Outlook 2010

Now that you have learned Quick Steps, we've surely gotten you excited about other ways you can automate your work. Another important time-saving feature is available using Quick Parts, which is similar to the AutoText feature in previous versions of Microsoft Office.

This is for you if you:

- Have a Word document with instructions that you copy and paste into email responses to your colleagues or customers.
- Have emails in your drafts folder that you call "email templates" and you use over and over again for colleagues and customers.
- Frequently provide email recipients links to your website, your department's web portal, parking instructions, podcast, etc..

- Want to instantly insert boiler plate content when composing emails.

For instance, suppose I work at Dunder Mifflin and I send interview candidates an email with standard instructions about what to expect, our website, our address, and directions/parking. In this example, I would create four Quick Parts. One Quick Part for each block of content. That way I can use the parking instructions Quick Part separately from the other Quick Parts, because sometimes I just need to send parking instructions and not the other stuff.

In this example, I'll include steps for creating the address and website Quick Parts.

To create a Quick Part response

1. Type the content in a blank email, such as the address to your office or parking instructions to your building.
2. Format the content so that it looks the way you want it. In one draft email, I typed several blocks of content that I planned to create Quick Parts for, as seen in Figure 241. **Note**: I added the URL for the word "website," by highlighting the word and using [CTRL]+[K] to add the hyperlink.

Figure 241. Quick Part examples drafted and formatted in an email

3. Select the content for the first Quick Part. In this example, I'm creating the Address Quick Part, so I only selected the address content as seen in Figure 242.

Figure 242. Selected content for my first Quick Part

4. With the text selected, click the **QUICK PARTS** drop-down in the **TEXT** group on the **INSERT** tab, and then select **SAVE SELECTION TO QUICK PART GALLERY…** as seen in Figure 243.

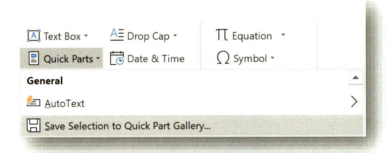

Figure 243. Save Selection to Quick Part Gallery… command on the Ribbon

5. This launches the **CREATE NEW BUILDING BLOCK** dialog box and places the first two words of your content in the **NAME** field, as seen in Figure 244.

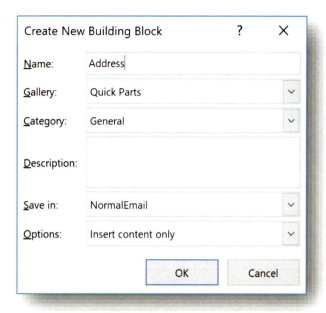

Figure 244. Name the Quick Part

6. Click **OK**.
7. To test out your new Quick Part, create a new message in Outlook and start typing the word **address** – it isn't case sensitive. As you type the word, you should see a tool tip pop up suggesting the Quick Part, as seen in Figure 245. Press [ENTER] to insert the full address.

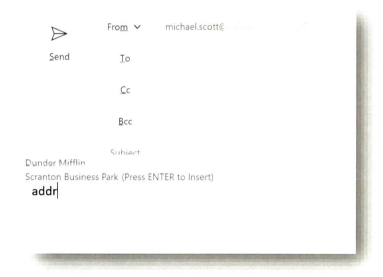

Figure 245. Tool tip for the address Quick Part

If the tool tip doesn't show up, click anywhere in the word and press [F3].

8. Now anytime you type **address**, you can replace those words with the full address automatically.

To create a Quick Part with a hyperlink

Next up, I want to create a Quick Part so that when I type the words **Visit our website** the word *website* automatically turns into a hyperlink in my emails.

1. Since I've already created the hyperlink in my email seen in Figure 246, I'm ready to save it as a Quick Part.

Figure 246. Quick Part examples drafted and formatted in an email

2. Select the hyperlinked word, as seen in Figure 247. Be sure to exclude any spaces after the word - you only want the hyperlinked word, no spaces.

246 © 2019 Vickie Sokol Evans, MCT The Red Cape Company. All Rights Reserved.

Visit our website for more information.

Figure 247. Selected hyperlink to save as a Quick Part

3. With the text selected, click the **QUICK PARTS** drop-down in the **TEXT** group on the **INSERT** tab and select **SAVE SELECTION TO QUICK PART GALLERY…** as seen in Figure 243.
4. This launches the **CREATE NEW BUILDING BLOCK** dialog box and places the first two words of your content in the **NAME** field. Keep the name and add **parking** at the end as seen in Figure 248.

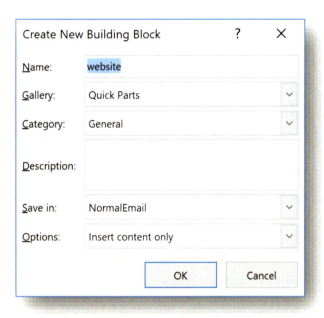

Figure 248. Name the hyperlink Quick Part

5. Click **OK**.
6. To test out your new Quick Part, create a new message in Outlook and start typing any phrase with the word *website* in it, such as **Visit our website** or **Here is the link to our website**. As you type the word *website*, you should see a tool tip pop up suggesting the website Quick Part as seen in Figure 249. Press [ENTER] to insert the hyperlink.

Figure 249. Tool tip for the hyperlink Quick Part

If the tool tip doesn't show up, click anywhere in the word and press [F3].

7. Repeat these steps for any hyperlink you use in your emails.

This tip meets a MOS certification exam objective.

Appendix

List of Figures

FIGURE 1. WINDOWS LOGO KEY ON A STANDARD KEYBOARD 1

FIGURE 2. WINDOW 10 START SCREEN 4

FIGURE 3. DEFAULT SEARCH RESULTS 7

FIGURE 4. SEARCH RESULTS FROM WINDOWS EXPLORER 8

FIGURE 5. USE WINDOWS EXPLORER TO FIND THE LARGEST FILES ON YOUR COMPUTER. 9

FIGURE 6. START MENU TASK BAR 10

FIGURE 7. CORTANA NOTEBOOK OPTIONS 11

FIGURE 8. WINDOWS 10 SYSTEM CLOCK WITH TWO ADDITIONAL TIME ZONES 12

FIGURE 9. "ADD CLOCKS FOR DIFFERENT TIME ZONES" SETTING 13

FIGURE 10. ADDITIONAL CLOCKS DIALOG BOX. 13

FIGURE 11. EXCEL JUMP LIST ON THE START MENU 15

FIGURE 12. NAMING YOUR NEW GROUP OF TILES ON THE START MENU 16

FIGURE 13. MY NAME IN THE TOP RIGHT-HAND CORNER OF MY APPLICATION WINDOW INDICATES I'M LOGGED INTO OFFICE 365.

.... 20

FIGURE 14. THE OFFICE 365 ACCOUNT PROFILE SCREEN WITHIN MICROSOFT OFFICE 21

FIGURE 15. CONNECTED SERVICES USING YOUR MICROSOFT OFFICE ACCOUNT(S) 22

FIGURE 16. OFFICE 2016 SAVE LOCATIONS 24

FIGURE 17. MY RECENT LIST IN THE WORD APP ON MY IPHONE 26

FIGURE 18. THE OPEN DIALOG BOX IN WORD 27

FIGURE 19. SHARING WINDOW IN WORD (OFFICE 365 FOR WORK/SCHOOL) 29

FIGURE 20. THE SHARE BUTTON IN MICROSOFT WORD 30

FIGURE 21. SHARING WINDOW IN WORD 31

FIGURE 22. LINK SETTINGS WHEN SHARING FILES WITH OTHERS 31

FIGURE 23. ADD THE RECIPIENT NAME OR EMAIL IN THE SEND LINK DIALOG BOX 33

FIGURE 24. COPY LINK OPTION IN THE SEND LINK DIALOG BOX 34

FIGURE 25. THE SEND TO OUTLOOK OPTION IN THE SEND LINK DIALOG BOX 34

FIGURE 26. SEND A COPY OF THE FILE 35

FIGURE 27. FILE > OPEN DIALOG BOX IN WORD SHOWING THE SHARED WITH ME OPTION 36

FIGURE 28. THE SHARED WITH ME AREA ON YOUR HOME PAGE WITHIN OFFICE 365 36

FIGURE 29. OFFICE 365 APPS LAUNCHER 37

FIGURE 30. THE ONEDRIVE APP LISTED AMONG OTHER OFFICE 365 APPS 37

FIGURE 31. CLICK SHARED WITHIN ONEDRIVE ONLINE TO VIEW FILES SHARED WITH YOU 38

FIGURE 32. CLICK SHARED WITHIN THE ONEDRIVE APP ON YOUR SMARTPHONE TO VIEW SHARED FILES 38

FIGURE 33. IMAGE OF THE ADDITIONAL EDITOR IN THIS FILE WITH ME 39

FIGURE 34. WORD MOBILE APP, CLICK THE ELLIPSIS (...) TO VIEW CO-AUTHORS 40

FIGURE 35. FROM MY MOBILE PHONE, I CAN SEE WHO ELSE IS EDITING THIS DOCUMENT 40

© 2019 Vickie Sokol Evans, MCT The Red Cape Company, LLC. All Rights Reserved.

FIGURE 36. THE AUTOSAVE FEATURE 41

FIGURE 37. COMMENT THREAD BETWEEN PAM AND ME 42

FIGURE 38. DOCUMENTS PINNED IN MICROSOFT WORD 43

FIGURE 39. DOCUMENTS AVAILABLE TO PIN TO THE OPEN SCREEN IN WORD................................. 44

FIGURE 40. QUICK ACCESS TOOLBAR 45

FIGURE 41. CUSTOMIZE QUICK ACCESS TOOLBAR WINDOW 46

FIGURE 42. MY CUSTOM RIBBON IN WORD.. 47

FIGURE 43. CUSTOMIZE RIBBON DIALOG BOX... 47

FIGURE 44. BRAND NEW RIBBON TAB AND GROUP BEFORE NAMING THEM 49

FIGURE 45. MY BOOK RIBBON TAB WITH FIVE NEW GROUPS (CUSTOM)..................................... 49

FIGURE 46. THE VIEW RIBBON TAB COMMANDS IN THE SHOW AND ZOOM GROUPS 50

FIGURE 47. THE FINISHED CUSTOM RIBBON TAB AS SEEN IN THE CUSTOMIZE RIBBON DIALOG BOX 51

FIGURE 48. RIBBON DISPLAY OPTIONS 52

FIGURE 49. KEY TIPS ACTIVATED 52

FIGURE 50. RESULTS FROM THE TELL ME FEATURE IN MICROSOFT WORD 53

FIGURE 51. RESULTS FROM THE TELL ME FEATURE IN MICROSOFT EXCEL 54

FIGURE 52. RESULTS FROM THE TELL ME FEATURE IN MICROSOFT POWERPOINT 55

FIGURE 53. THE TELL ME SEARCH FIELD IN WORD.. 55

FIGURE 54. CLICK THE MORE BUTTON TO REVEAL COLORS PALETTES FOR YOUR PRESENTATION. 57

FIGURE 55. CREATE NEW THEME COLORS DIALOG BOX 58

FIGURE 56. BACKSTAGE WINDOW – CREATE A PDF USING EXPORT 62

FIGURE 57. BACKSTAGE WINDOW: EMAIL AS A PDF... 63

FIGURE 58. BACKSTAGE VIEW: DOCUMENT PROPERTIES 66

FIGURE 59. DOCUMENT INSPECTOR FOR WORD 67

FIGURE 60. SELECTION ARROW 69

FIGURE 61. APPLY THE TITLE STYLE TO THE TITLE OF THE DOCUMENT. 70

FIGURE 62. STYLES GALLERY "MORE" BUTTON 71

FIGURE 63. SELECT ALL TEXT WITH SIMILAR FORMATTING (NO DATA)...................................... 73

FIGURE 64. CHANGE STYLE SET 74

FIGURE 65. MODIFY STYLE DIALOG BOX... 75

FIGURE 66. TABLE OF CONTENTS MENU ON THE RIBBON... 76

FIGURE 67. TABLE OF CONTENTS WINDOW... 77

FIGURE 68. THE SHOW/HIDE PARAGRAPH MARKS COMMAND ON THE HOME RIBBON.................. 80

FIGURE 69. THE MORE BUTTON IN THE FIND AND REPLACE DIALOG BOX 80

FIGURE 70. FIND AND REPLACE MORE DIALOG BOX.. 81

FIGURE 71. TABLE TOOLS CONTEXTUAL TABS ON THE RIBBON 83

FIGURE 72. THE TABLE STYLES "MORE" BUTTON ON THE TABLE DESIGN RIBBON 83

FIGURE 73. NAVIGATION PANE RIGHT-CLICK MENU 87

FIGURE 74. DRAG THE FILL HANDLE ON THE CELL TO AUTOFILL THE SERIES. 90

FIGURE 75. AUTOFILL TIME USING A SPECIFIC INCREMENT 91

FIGURE 76. USE THE FILL HANDLE TO COPY CALCULATIONS.. 92

FIGURE 77. USE THE CORNER BUTTON TO SELECT THE ENTIRE WORKSHEET. 93

FIGURE 78. ENTIRE WORKSHEET IS SELECTED. 94

FIGURE 79. FORMAT AS TABLE DIALOG BOX 97

FIGURE 80. TABLE STYLES MORE BUTTON 98

FIGURE 81. TABLE AUTOEXPANSION DIALOG BOX 99

250   © 2019 Vickie Sokol Evans, MCT The Red Cape Company. All Rights Reserved.

FIGURE 82. AUTOCALCULATION OPTIONS BUTTON...100

FIGURE 83. TURN OFF AUTOCALCULATED COLUMNS FOR ALL WORKBOOKS...........................101

FIGURE 84. WITHIN A TOTAL ROW CELL, CLICK THE DROP-DOWN BOX TO REVEAL POPULAR FUNCTIONS.............................102

FIGURE 85. TWO SLICERS ADDED FOR THE TRAVEL & EXPENSES TABLE 103

FIGURE 86. SELECT DATA IN A TABLE COLUMN 104

FIGURE 87. HOW TO SELECT ALL THE DATA IN A TABLE COLUMN AT ONCE. 105

FIGURE 88. REMOVE DUPLICATES DIALOG BOX..106

FIGURE 89. EXAMPLE PIVOTTABLE OF MONTHLY BILLABLE EXPENSE BY CLIENT PROJECTS 107

FIGURE 90. CREATE PIVOTTABLE DIALOG BOX 107

FIGURE 91. THE PIVOTTABLE BUILDER FOR BILLABLE CLIENT EXPENSE REPORT......................108

FIGURE 92. THE CLEAR OPTIONS AVAILABLE 109

FIGURE 93. THE STATUS BAR DISPLAYS THE AUTOCALCULATE VALUES 110

FIGURE 94. THE CUSTOMIZE STATUS BAR WINDOW SHOWING THE AUTOCALCULATE OPTIONS 111

FIGURE 95. COLUMN OF FULL NAMES THAT NEED TO BE SEPARATED 112

FIGURE 96. CONVERT TEXT TO COLUMNS WIZARD - STEP 1 OF 3: SELECT DELIMITED 113

FIGURE 97. CONVERT TO TEXT COLUMNS WIZARD - STEP 2 OF 3: CHOOSE YOUR DELIMITER, SUCH AS SPACE 113

FIGURE 98. CONVERT TEXT TO COLUMNS WIZARD - STEP 3 OF 3: CONFIRM DATA TYPE FORMAT.........114

FIGURE 99. THE RANGE SELECTED USING [CTRL]+[A] CONFIRMS COLUMN D IS MY FIRST BLANK COLUMN, WHICH CAN BE DELETED.........115

FIGURE 100. USE A COLUMN'S FILTER BUTTON TO CHECK FOR DATA IN THAT COLUMN. 115

FIGURE 101. THE PASTE DROP-DOWN MENU 117

FIGURE 102. PASTE SPECIAL DIALOG BOX...118

FIGURE 103. NEW FORMATTING RULE DIALOG BOX FOR FINDING DUPLICATE VALUES IN A RANGE OF CELLS 120

FIGURE 104. SORT BY CELL COLOR USING THE SORT & FILTER OPTIONS AVAILABLE ON THE EMAIL COLUMN.........121

FIGURE 105. EXCEL SORTED THE DUPLICATES TO THE TOP OF THE LIST WHILE KEEPING THE OTHER CONTACTS SORTED BY LAST NAME.........122

FIGURE 106. FILTER BY CELL COLOR USING SORT & FILTER OPTIONS AVAILABLE ON THE EMAIL COLUMN. 122

FIGURE 107. FILTERED LIST TO ONLY SHOW THE ROWS WITH DUPLICATE VALUES IN A COLUMN.........123

FIGURE 108. EXAMPLE STATUS FLAGS WITH CONDITIONAL FORMATTING 124

FIGURE 109. NEW FORMATTING RULE DIALOG BOX FOR CONDITIONAL FORMATTING BASED ON CELLS THAT CONTAIN SPECIFIC TEXT 125

FIGURE 110. CHOOSE CUSTOM FORMAT... FROM THE FORMAT WITH... DROP-DOWN. 125

FIGURE 111 CHANGE THE BACKGROUND COLOR TO A STANDARD COLOR GREEN. 126

FIGURE 112. EXAMPLE HEAT MAP COMPARED TO A REPORT WITHOUT A HEAT MAP 127

FIGURE 113. HEAT MAP OPTIONS USING COLOR SCALES CONDITIONAL FORMATTING..............128

FIGURE 114. RECOMMENDED CHARTS FOR THE SALES DATA SELECTED 129

FIGURE 115. THE QUICK ANALYSIS TOOL 130

FIGURE 116. A PREVIEW OF THE LINE CHART USING THE QUICK ANALYSIS TOOL 131

FIGURE 117. REPORT WITHOUT SPARKLINES 131

FIGURE 118. REPORT WITH SPARKLINES...132

FIGURE 119. EXAMPLE REPORT WITH COLUMN SPARKLINES 132

FIGURE 120. CREATE SPARKLINES DIALOG BOX 133

FIGURE 121. PAGE WIDTH SETTINGS ON THE PAGE LAYOUT TAB 134

FIGURE 122. PRINT PREVIEW SETTINGS FOR PAGE ORIENTATION AND MARGINS....................135

FIGURE 123. PAGE AND HEIGHT WIDTH SET TO PRINT ON ONE PAGE 135

FIGURE 124. FIT SHEET ON ONE PAGE SCALING OPTION IN THE PRINT WINDOW 136

© 2019 Vickie Sokol Evans, MCT The Red Cape Company, LLC. All Rights Reserved.   251

FIGURE 125. PRINT TITLES COMMAND ON THE PAGE LAYOUT RIBBON 137

FIGURE 126. PRINT TITLES SETTING IN THE PAGE SETUP DIALOG BOX 137

FIGURE 127. MOVE OR COPY WORKSHEET DIALOG BOX: THIS OPTION MUST BE CHECKED 138

FIGURE 128. THEMES GALLERY SHOWING MY CUSTOM THEMES 142

FIGURE 129. SELECTING THE "BANDED" THEME FOR MY PRESENTATION 143

FIGURE 130. VARIANTS AVAILABLE FOR THE "BANDED" THEME 143

FIGURE 131. THE VARIANT I CHOSE FOR THE "BANDED" THEME 144

FIGURE 132. COLOR SETS AVAILABLE IN POWERPOINT 145

FIGURE 133. THE RED VIOLET COLOR SET APPLIED TO THE "BANDED" THEME 145

FIGURE 134. FONT SETS AVAILABLE IN POWERPOINT 146

FIGURE 135. SECTION COMMANDS AVAILABLE WHEN YOU RIGHT-CLICK A SECTION 150

FIGURE 136. PRINT DIALOG BOX TO PRINT SECTIONS 151

FIGURE 137. SUMMARY SLIDE EXAMPLE USING THE NEW ZOOM FEATURE..152

FIGURE 138. INSERT SUMMARY ZOOM COMMAND ON THE INSERT RIBBON 153

FIGURE 139. INSERT SUMMARY ZOOM DIALOG BOX WITH SECTION HEADER SLIDES SELECTED 153

FIGURE 140. NEW SUMMARY SECTION AND SUMMARY ZOOM SLIDE 154

FIGURE 141. THE NEW SUMMARY ZOOM SLIDE 154

FIGURE 142. ZOOM STYLES 155

FIGURE 143. THE FINAL VERSION OF MY SUMMARY ZOOM 155

FIGURE 144. RETURN TO ZOOM CHECK BOX ON THE ZOOM TOOLS FORMAT TAB 156

FIGURE 145. EDIT SUMMARY COMMAND ON THE ZOOM TOOLS FORMAT TAB 156

FIGURE 146. DEFINE CUSTOM SLIDE SHOW DIALOG BOX 157

FIGURE 147. STANDARD SLIDE LAYOUTS FOR A POWERPOINT THEME 158

FIGURE 148. NEW SLIDE DROP-DOWN TO VIEW AVAILABLE LAYOUTS 159

FIGURE 149. LAYOUT DROP-DOWN TO CHANGE EXISTING LAYOUT TO A DIFFERENT LAYOUT 160

FIGURE 150. THE POWERPOINT RESET BUTTON 161

FIGURE 151. SLIDE MASTER AND CORRESPONDING LAYOUTS 162

FIGURE 152. CHANGING BULLETS ON OUR SLIDE MASTER 163

FIGURE 153. EXAMPLE CUSTOM SLIDE LAYOUT FOR THE TEAM 164

FIGURE 154. THE 8 TYPES OF PLACEHOLDERS YOU CAN ADD TO A SLIDE 165

FIGURE 155. THE INSERT PLACEHOLDER DROP-DOWN MENU...166

FIGURE 156. CONVERT TO SMARTART 168

FIGURE 157. SMARTART GALLERY 169

FIGURE 158. SMARTART TEXT HANDLE 169

FIGURE 159. THE MORE BUTTON IN THE TRANSITION TO THIS SLIDE GROUP. 170

FIGURE 160. REMOVE BACKGROUND BUTTON 172

FIGURE 161. REMOVE BACKGROUND FEATURE 173

FIGURE 162. REMOVE BACKGROUND COMMANDS...173

FIGURE 163. DRAW A STRAIGHT LINE THROUGH THE AREA YOU WANT TO REMOVE. 174

FIGURE 164. DRAW A STRAIGHT LINE THROUGH THE AREA YOU WANT TO KEEP 174

FIGURE 165. THE "MORE" BUTTON IN THE PICTURE STYLES GROUP..175

FIGURE 166. DYNAMIC CONNECTION OF SHAPES 177

FIGURE 167. DESIGN IDEAS FOR THE NEW IMAGE ON A SLIDE...179

FIGURE 168. EXAMPLE DESIGN IDEA USING THE DESIGNER TOOL 179

FIGURE 169. SHOW PRESENTER VIEW DURING A SLIDE SHOW 181

FIGURE 170. PRESENTER VIEW OPTIONS WITHIN PRESENTER VIEW 182

252   © 2019 Vickie Sokol Evans, MCT The Red Cape Company. All Rights Reserved.

FIGURE 171. PRESENTER VIEW - MOVE THROUGH SLIDES 182

FIGURE 172. PRESENTER VIEW - POINT OR WRITE ON SLIDES 182

FIGURE 173. PRESENTER VIEW – SEE ALL SLIDES (AND SECTIONS!) 183

FIGURE 174. PRESENTER VIEW - ZOOM INTO THE SLIDE 183

FIGURE 175. PRESENTER VIEW – BLACK OR UNBLACK SLIDE SHOW 183

FIGURE 176. PRESENTER VIEW - MORE SLIDE SHOW OPTIONS 184

FIGURE 177. POWERPOINT 2007/2010 PRESENTER VIEW 184

FIGURE 178. SLIDE SHOW ZOOM COMMAND 185

FIGURE 179. POWERPOINT RECORDING TOOLS 186

FIGURE 180. POWERPOINT VIDEO RIGHT-CLICK MENUS 189

FIGURE 181. TRIM VIDEO WINDOW 190

FIGURE 182. CLEAN UP BUTTON 193

FIGURE 183. CLEAN UP FOLDER CONFIRMATION 193

FIGURE 184. CLEAN UP FOLDER - OUTLOOK OPTIONS DIALOG BOX 194

FIGURE 185. CLEAN UP FOLDER SETTINGS - SELECT FOLDER 194

FIGURE 186. CLEAN UP SETTINGS 195

FIGURE 187. CLEAN UP BUTTON 196

FIGURE 188. CLEAN UP FOLDER CONFIRMATION 196

FIGURE 189. THE IGNORE BUTTON ON THE HOME RIBBON 198

FIGURE 190. REPLY WITH MEETING BUTTON 199

FIGURE 191. TIME ZONES COMMAND IN OUTLOOK 201

FIGURE 192. TIME ZONES COMMAND IN THE OUTLOOK RIBBON IN PREVIOUS VERSION 201

FIGURE 193. TIME ZONES SET FOR HOUSTON (IAH AIRPORT) TO LONDON (LHR AIRPORT) FLIGHT 201

FIGURE 194. DATE & TIME SETTING FOR WINDOWS 10 202

FIGURE 195. WINDOWS DATE AND TIME DIALOG BOX FOR PREVIOUS VERSIONS OF WINDOWS 202

FIGURE 196. ACTIVE HYPERLINKS FOR PHONE AND ADDRESSES ON A MOBILE DEVICE 203

FIGURE 197. COMPARE ADDRESS FORMATS ON RECIPIENT'S SMARTPHONE 205

FIGURE 198. RECENT ITEMS LIST FOR OUTLOOK ATTACHMENTS 207

FIGURE 199. ATTACHMENT STATUS FOR OFFICE 365 ATTACHMENTS 208

FIGURE 200. ATTACHMENTS OPTIONS FOR LINK ATTACHMENTS 208

FIGURE 201. PERMISSION OPTIONS FOR LINK ATTACHMENTS 209

FIGURE 202. INBOX FILTERS FOR OUTLOOK > FILTER FOR MENTIONED MAIL 211

FIGURE 203. RECIPIENT'S EMAIL WITH @MENTIONS 212

FIGURE 204. EXAMPLE OF MIXED FORMATS WHEN REPURPOSING CONTENT 213

FIGURE 205. BAD EXAMPLE OF RESENDING A MESSAGE. 214

FIGURE 206. CLEAR ALL FORMATTING BUTTON. 214

FIGURE 207. THE RESEND COMMAND ON THE ACTIONS DROP-DOWN MENU 215

FIGURE 208. EXPIRED MESSAGE FROM KAREN BERG SITTING IN AN INBOX 216

FIGURE 209. DIALOG BOX LAUNCHER FOR MORE OPTIONS 216

FIGURE 210. EXPIRES AFTER SETTING FOR MESSAGES 217

FIGURE 211. DIRECT REPLIES TO COMMAND ON THE RIBBON 217

FIGURE 212. HAVE REPLIES SENT TO OPTION 218

FIGURE 213. SEARCH RIBBON IN OUTLOOK 219

FIGURE 214. OUTLOOK SEARCH BAR 220

FIGURE 215. OUTLOOK SEARCH RIBBON 220

FIGURE 216. DEFAULT SEARCH FOLDERS IN THE MAILBOX FOLDER LIST 222

© 2019 Vickie Sokol Evans, MCT The Red Cape Company, LLC. All Rights Reserved.   253

FIGURE 217. NEW SEARCH FOLDER 223

FIGURE 218. CUSTOM SEARCH FOLDER DIALOG BOX.. 223

FIGURE 219. SELECT NAMES DIALOG BOX FOR THE SEARCH FOLDER 224

FIGURE 220. THE "FROM" SETTING FOR SEARCH FOLDERS.. 224

FIGURE 221. MORE CHOICES TAB IN THE SEARCH FOLDER CRITERIA DIALOG BOX.................. 225

FIGURE 222. OUTLOOK CONDITIONAL FORMATTING FONT DIALOG BOX 226

FIGURE 223. CONDITIONAL FORMATTING DIALOG BOX IN OUTLOOK 227

FIGURE 224. SELECT NAMES DIALOG BOX 227

FIGURE 225. FILTER SETTINGS FOR THE CONDITIONAL FORMAT... 228

FIGURE 226. CONDITIONAL FORMATTING APPLIED TO MICHAEL SCOTT'S EMAILS 228

FIGURE 227. CONDITIONAL FORMATTING RULES 229

FIGURE 228. CREATE RULES DIALOG BOX 230

FIGURE 229. CREATE A RULE USING THE RULES WIZARD... 231

FIGURE 230. RULES WIZARD STEP 1 232

FIGURE 231. RULES WIZARD SET ACTION 233

FIGURE 232. SETTING THE ACTION TO FOLLOW UP TODAY 234

FIGURE 233. FINAL STEP OF RULES WIZARD 235

FIGURE 234. DEFAULT QUICK STEPS 237

FIGURE 235. FIRST TIME SETUP DIALOG BOX FOR TEAM EMAIL QUICK STEP........................ 238

FIGURE 236. CLICK THE OPTIONS BUTTON TO CONFIGURE YOUR QUICK STEPS 239

FIGURE 237. EMAIL ADDRESSES ADDED TO THE TEAM EMAIL FIRST TIME SETUP DIALOG BOX........................ 239

FIGURE 238. EDIT QUICK STEP DIALOG BOX... 240

FIGURE 239. EDIT QUICK STEP EMAIL OPTIONS 241

FIGURE 240. FIRST TIME SETUP DIALOG BOX FOR TEAM EMAIL QUICK STEP 242

FIGURE 241. QUICK PART EXAMPLES DRAFTED AND FORMATTED IN AN EMAIL 243

FIGURE 242. SELECTED CONTENT FOR MY FIRST QUICK PART 244

FIGURE 243. SAVE SELECTION TO QUICK PART GALLERY... COMMAND ON THE RIBBON....... 244

FIGURE 244. NAME THE QUICK PART 245

FIGURE 245. TOOL TIP FOR THE ADDRESS QUICK PART 245

FIGURE 246. QUICK PART EXAMPLES DRAFTED AND FORMATTED IN AN EMAIL 246

FIGURE 247. SELECTED HYPERLINK TO SAVE AS A QUICK PART 247

FIGURE 248. NAME THE HYPERLINK QUICK PART 247

FIGURE 249. TOOL TIP FOR THE HYPERLINK QUICK PART 248